Report Writing for Data Science in R

Roger D. Peng

Report Writing for Data Science in R

Roger D. Peng

This book is for sale at http://leanpub.com/reportwriting

This version was published on 2015-12-03

Leanpub

This is a Leanpub book. Leanpub empowers authors and publishers with the Lean Publishing process. Lean Publishing is the act of publishing an in-progress ebook using lightweight tools and many iterations to get reader feedback, pivot until you have the right book and build traction once you do.

©2015 Roger D. Peng

Also By Roger D. Peng

R Programming for Data Science

The Art of Data Science

Exploratory Data Analysis with R

Contents

Stay in Touch! 1

Getting Started with R 3

What is Reproducible Reporting? 5

The Data Science Pipeline 13

Literate Statistical Programming 17

Organizing a Data Analysis 21

Structure of a Data Analysis: Part 1 29

Structure of a Data Analysis: Part 2 37

Markdown 55

Using knitr for Reproducible Reports 63

Communicating Results Over E-mail 85

Reproducibility Check List 91

Evidence-based Data Analysis 103

Public Reproducibility Resources 119

Stay in Touch!

Thanks for purchasing this book. If you are interested in hearing more from me about things that I'm working on (books, data science courses, podcast, etc.), you can do two things.

First, I encourage you to join my mailing list of Leanpub Readers[1]. On this list I send out updates of my own activities as well as occasional comments on data science current events. I'll also let you know what my co-conspirators Jeff Leek and Brian Caffo are up to because sometimes they do really cool stuff.

Second, I have a regular podcast called Not So Standard Deviations[2] that I co-host with Dr. Hilary Parker, a Senior Data Analyst at Etsy. On this podcast, Hilary and I talk about the craft of data science and discuss common issues and problems in analyzing data. We'll also compare how data science is approached in both academia and industry contexts and discuss the latest industry trends.

You can listen to recent episodes on our SoundCloud page or you can subscribe to it in iTunes[3] or your favorite podcasting app.

Thanks again for purchasing this book and please do stay in touch!

---

[1] http://eepurl.com/bAJ3zj
[2] https://soundcloud.com/nssd-podcast
[3] https://itunes.apple.com/us/podcast/not-so-standard-deviations/id1040614570

Getting Started with R

Installation

The first thing you need to do to get started with R is to install it on your computer. R works on pretty much every platform available, including the widely available Windows, Mac OS X, and Linux systems. If you want to watch a step-by-step tutorial on how to install R for Mac or Windows, you can watch these videos:

- Installing R on Windows[4]
- Installing R on the Mac[5]

There is also an integrated development environment available for R that is built by RStudio. I really like this IDE—it has a nice editor with syntax highlighting, there is an R object viewer, and there are a number of other nice features that are integrated. You can see how to install RStudio here

- Installing RStudio[6]

The RStudio IDE is available from RStudio's web site[7].

---
[4] http://youtu.be/Ohnk9hcxf9M
[5] https://youtu.be/uxuuWXU-7UQ
[6] https://youtu.be/bM7Sfz-LADM
[7] http://rstudio.com

Getting started with the R interface

After you install R you will need to launch it and start writing R code. Before we get to exactly how to write R code, it's useful to get a sense of how the system is organized. In these two videos I talk about where to write code and how set your working directory, which let's R know where to find all of your files.

- Writing code and setting your working directory on the Mac[8]
- Writing code and setting your working directory on Windows[9]

---

[8] https://youtu.be/8xT3hmJQskU
[9] https://youtu.be/XBcvH1BpIBo

What is Reproducible Reporting?

Watch a video of this chapter.[10]

This chapter will be about reproducible reporting, and I want to take the opportunity to cover some basic concepts and ideas that are related to reproducible reporting, just in case you haven't heard about it or don't know what it is.

Before we get to *reproducibility*, we need to cover a little background with respect to how science works (even if you're not a scientist, this is important). The basic idea is that in science, *replication* is the most important element of verifying and validating findings. So if you claim that X causes Y, or that Vitamin C improves disease, or that something causes a problem, what happens is that other scientists that are independent of you will try to investigate that same question and see if they come up with a similar result. If lots of different people come up with the same result and replicate the original finding, then we tend to think that the original finding was probably true and that this is a real relationship or real finding.

The ultimate standard in strengthening scientific evidence is replication. The goal is to have independent people to do independent things with different data, different methods, and different laboratories and see if you get the same result. There's a sense that if a relationship in nature is truly there, then it should be robust to having different people discover it in different ways. Replication is particularly important

---

[10] https://www.youtube.com/watch?v=4rBX6r5emgQ

in areas where findings can have big policy impacts or can influence regulatory types of decisions.

What's Wrong with Replication?

What's wrong with replication? There's really nothing wrong with it. This is what science has been doing for a long time, through hundreds of years. And there's nothing wrong with it today. But the problem is that it's becoming more and more challenging to do replication or to replicate other studies. Part of the reason is because studies are getting bigger and bigger.

In order to do big studies you need a lot of money and so, well, there's a lot of money involved! If you want to do ten versions of the same study, you need ten times as much money and there's not as much money around as there used to be. Sometimes it's difficult to replicate a study because if the original study took 20 years to do, it's difficult to wait around another 20 years for replication. Some studies are just plain unique, such as studying the impact of a massive earthquake in a very specific location and time. If you're looking at a unique situation in time or a unique population, you can't readily replicate that situation.

There are a lot of good reasons why you can't replicate a study. If you can't replicate a study, is the alternative just to do nothing, just let that study stand by itself? The idea behind a reproducible reporting is to create a kind of minimum standard or a middle ground where we won't be replicating a study, but maybe we can do something in between. The basic problem is that you have the gold standard, which is replication, and then you have the worst standard which is doing nothing. What can we do that's in between the gold standard and diong nothing? That is where reproducibility comes in. That's how we can kind of bridge the gap between replication and nothing.

In non-research settings, often full replication isn't even the point. Often the goal is to preserve something to the point where anybody in an organization can repeat what you did (for example, after you leave the organization). In this case, reproducibility is key to maintaining the history of a project and making sure that every step along the way is clear.

Reproducibility to the Rescue

Why do we need this kind of middle ground? I haven't clearly defined reproducibility yet, but the basic idea is that you need to make the **data** available for the original study and the **computational methods** available so that other people can look at your data and run the kind of analysis that you've run, and come to the same findings that you found.

What reproducible reporting is about is a *validation of the data analysis*. Because you're not collecting independent data using independent methods, it's a little bit more difficult to validate the scientific question itself. But if you can take someone's data and reproduce their findings, then you can, in some sense, validate the data analysis. This involves having the data and the code because more likely than not, the analysis will have been done on the computer using some sort of programming language, like R. So you can take their code and their data and reproduce the findings that they come up with. Then you can at least have confidence that the analysis was done appropriately and that the correct methods were used.

Recently, there's been a lot of discussion of reproducibility in the media and in the scientific literature. The journal

Science had a special issue on reproducibility and data replication. Other journals of updated policies on publication to encourage reproducibility. In 2012, a feature on the TV show 60 minutes looked at a major incident at Duke University where many results involving a promising cancer test were found to be not reproducible. This led to a number of studies and clinical trials having to be stopped, followed by a investigation which is still ongoing.

Finally, the Institute of Medicine, in response to a lot of recent events involving reproducibility of scientific studies, issued a report saying that best practices should be done to promote and encourage reproducibility, particularly in what's called 'omics based research, such as genomics, proteomics, other similar areas involving high-throughput biological measurements. This was a very important report. Of the many recommendations that the IOM made, the key ones were that

- Data and metadata need to be made available;
- Computer code should be fully specified, so that people can examine it to see what was done;
- All the steps of the computational analysis, including any preprocessing of data, should be fully described so that people can study it and reproduce it.

From "X" to "Computational X"

What is driving this need for a "reproducibility middle ground" between replication and doing nothing? For starters, there are a lot of new technologies on the scene and in many different fields of study including, biology, chemistry and environmental science. These technologies allow us to collect data at a much higher throughput so we end up with these very complex and very high dimensional data sets. These datasets can be collected almost instantaneously compared to even just ten years ago—the technology has allowed us to create huge data sets at essentially the touch of a button. Furthermore, we the computing power to take existing (already huge) databases and merge them into even bigger and bigger databases. Finally, the massive increase in computing power has allowed us to implement more sophisticated and complex analysis routines.

The analyses themselves, the models that we fit and the algorithms that we run, are much much more complicated than they used to be. Having a basic understanding of these algorithms is difficult, even for a sophisticated person, and it's almost impossible to describe these algorithms with words alone. Understanding what someone did in a data analysis now requires looking at *code* and scrutinizing the computer programs that people used.

The bottom line with all these different trends is that for every field "X", there is now "Computational X". There's computational biology, computational astronomy—whatever it is you want, there is a computational version of it.

Air Pollution and Health: A Perfect Storm

One example of an area were reproducibility is important comes from research that I've conducted in the area of air pollution and health. Air pollution and health is a big field and it involves a confluence of features that emphasize the need for reproducibility.

The first feature is that we're estimating very small, but very important, public health effects in the presence of a numerous much stronger signals. You can think about air pollution as something that's perhaps harmful, but even if it were harmful there are likely many other things that are going to be more harmful that you have to worry about. Pollution is going to be at the very top of the list of things that are going to harm you. In other words, there's an inherently weak signal there.

Second, the results of a lot of air pollution research inform substantial policy decisions. Many federal air pollution regulations in the United States are based on scientific research in this area and these regulations can affect a lot of stakeholders in government and industry.

Finally, we use a lot of complex statistical methods to do these studies and these statistical methods are subsequently subjected to intense scrutiny. The combination of an inherently weak signal, substantial policy impacts, and complex statistical methods almost require that the research that we do be reproducible.

One of the things that we've done here at Johns Hopkins is to create what's called the Internet-based Health and Air Pollution Surveillance System[11] (iHAPSS). We make a lot of our data available, our statistical methods are distributed in the form of R code and R packages so that they can be examined, and the data and many of the results from our papers are available so that they can be reproduced by others.

Summary

- Replication, whereby scientific questions are examined and verified independently by different scientists, is the gold standard for scientific validity.

---

[11] http://www.ihapss.jhsph.edu

- Replication can be difficult and often there are no resources to independently replicate a study.
- Reproducibility, whereby data and code are re-analyzed by independent scientists to obtain the same results of the original investigator, is a reasonable minimum standard when replication is not possible.

The Data Science Pipeline

Watch a video of this chapter.[12]

The basic issue is when you read a description of a data analysis, such as in an article or a technical report, for the most part, what you get is the report and nothing else. Of course, everyone knows that behind the scenes there's *a lot* that went into this report and that's what I call the **data science pipeline**.

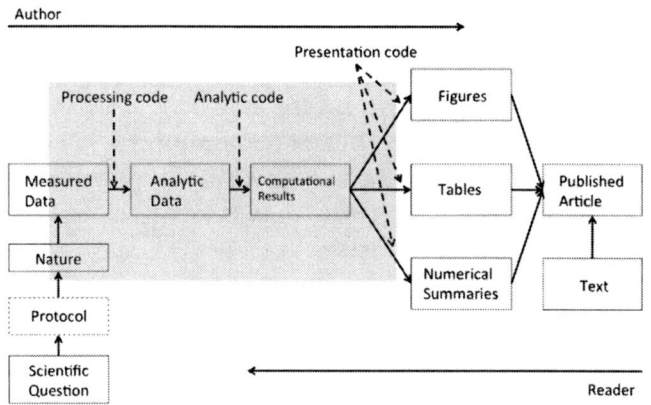

The Data Science Pipeline

In this pipeline, there are two "actors": the *author* of the report/article and the *reader*. On the left side, the author is going from left to right along this pipeline. The reader is going from right to left. If you're the reader you read the article and you want to know more about what happened: Where is the data? What was used here? The basic idea

---

[12] https://www.youtube.com/watch?v=GXSRP--d3Q4

behind reproducibility is to focus on the elements in the blue blox: the analytic data and the computational results. With reproducibility the goal is to allow the author of a report and the reader of that report to "meet in the middle".

Elements of Reproducibility

What do we need for reproducibility? There's a variety of ways to talk about this, but one basic definition that we've come up with is that there are four things that are required to make results reproducible:

1. **Analytic data**. The data that were used for the analysis that was presented should be available for others to access. This is different from the *raw data* because very often in a data analysis the raw data are not all used for the analysis, but rather some subset is used. It may be interesting to see the raw data but impractical to actually have it. Analytic data is key to examining the data analysis.
2. **Analytic code**. The analytic code is the code that was applied to the analytic data to produce the key results. This may be preprocessing code, regression modeling code, or really any other code used to produce the results from the analytic data.
3. **Documentation**. Documentation of that code and the data is very important.
4. **Distribution**. Finally, there needs to be some standard means of distribution, so all this data in the code is easily accessible.

Authors and Readers

It is important to realize that there are multiple players when you talk about reproducibility–there are different types of parties that have different types of interests. There are authors who produce research and they want to make their research reproducible. There are also readers of research and they want to reproduce that work. Everyone needs tools to make their lives easier.

One current challenge is that authors of research have to undergo considerable effort to make their results available to a wide audience. Publishing data and code today is not necessarily a trivial task. Although there are a number of resources available now, that were not available even five years ago, it's still a bit of a challenge to get things out on the web (or at least distributed widely). Resources like GitHub[13] and RPubs[14] and various data repositories have made a big difference, but there is still a ways to go with respect to building up the public reproducibility infrastructure.

Furthermore, even when data and code are available, readers often have to download the data, download the code, and then they have to piece everything together, usually by hand. It's not always an easy task to put the data and code together. Also, readers may not have the same computational resources that the original authors did. If the original authors used an enormous computing cluster, for example, to do their analysis, the readers may not have that same enormous computing cluster at their disposal. It may be difficult for readers to reproduce the same results.

Generally the toolbox for doing reproducible research is small, although it's definitely growing. In practice, authors

---

[13] https://github.com
[14] http://rpubs.com

often just throw things up on the web. There are journals and supplementary materials, but they are famously disorganized. There are only a few central databases that authors can take advantage of to post their data and make it available. So if you're working in a field that has a central database that everyone uses, that's great. If you're not, then you have to assemble your own resources.

Summary

- The process of conducting and disseminating research can be depicted as a "data science pipeline"
- Readers and consumers of data science research are typically not privy to the details of the data science pipeline
- One view of reproducibility is that it gives research consumers partial access to the raw pipeline elements.

Literate Statistical Programming

Watch a video of this chapter.[15]

One basic idea to make writing reproducible reports easier is what's known as *literate statistical programming* (or sometimes called literate statistical practice[16]). This comes from the idea of literate programming[17] in the area of writing computer programs.

The idea is to think of a report or a publication as a stream of text and code. The text is readable by people and the code is readable by computers. The analysis is described in a series of text and code chunks. Each kind of code chunk will do something like load some data or compute some results. Each text chunk will relay something in a human readable language. There might also be presentation code that formats tables and figures and there's article text that explains what's going on around all this code. This stream of text and code is a literate statistical program or a literate statistical analysis.

Weaving and Tangling

Literate programs by themselves are a bit difficult to work with, but they can be processed in two important ways. Literate programs can be **weaved** to produce human readable

---

[15] https://www.youtube.com/watch?v=bwQWhZQmDuc
[16] http://www.r-project.org/conferences/DSC-2001/Proceedings/Rossini.pdf
[17] https://en.wikipedia.org/wiki/Literate_programming

documents like PDFs or HTML web pages, and they can **tangled** to produce machine-readable "documents", or in other words, machine readable code. The basic idea behind literate programming in order to generate the different kinds of output you might need, you only need a *single source document*—you can weave and tangle to get the rist. In order to use a system like this you need a documentational language, that's human readable, and you need a programming language that's machine readable (or can be compiled/interpreted into something that's machine readable).

Sweave

One of the original literate programming systems in R that was designed to do this was called Sweave. Sweave uses a documentation program called LaTeX and a programming language, which obviously is R. It was originally developed by Fritz Leisch, who is a core member of R, and the code base is still maintained by R Core. The Sweave system comes with a any installation of R.

There are many limitations to the original Sweave system. One of the limitations is that it is focused primarily on LaTeX, which is not a documentation language that many people are familiar with. Therefore, it can be difficult to learn this type of markup language if you're not already in a field that uses it regularly. Sweave also lacks a lot of features that people find useful like caching, and multiple plots per page and mixing programming languages.

knitr

One of the alternative that has come up in recent times is something called `knitr`. The `knitr` package for R takes a lot of these ideas of literate programming and updates and improves upon them. knitr still uses R as its programming language, but it allows you to mix other programming languages in. You can also use a variety of documentation languages now, such as LaTeX, markdown and HTML. knitr was developed by Yihui Xie while he was a graduate student at Iowa State and it has become a very popular package for writing literate statistical programs.

Summary

- Literate statistical programming tools can make it easier to write up reproducible documents containing data analyses.
- Sweave was one of the first literate statistical programming tools, which weaved together a statistical language (R) with a markup language (LaTeX).
- knitr is a package that builds on the work of Sweave and provides much more powerful functionality, including the ability to write in Markdown and create a variety of output formats.

Organizing a Data Analysis

In this chapter, I'm going to give a couple of basic notes on how to organize a data analysis. Of course, there's no universal way to do this that would apply to every single data analysis performed by anybody in the world, but I think there's some useful tips that can be used to help you put things together in logical places and ultimately ensure that your data analysis is reproducible either by yourself or by someone else.

Files Files Files...

The kind of key data analysis files that you will retain over the course of a major project are going to be raw data and processed data and you're probably going to want to save a lot of this in various places. You'll generate some figures or tables, for example, and they're going to be exploratory figures that you put together to look at the data to produce this rough cut of what the data analysis might look like. These exploratory figures are not going to be very polished. They'll be just good enough to get you a sense of what the data look like. Then there might be some final figures. These final figures are going to be useful for you to put in reports. These are the figures you're going to show to other people, they're going to be well annotated and nicely organized and put together.

Of course, there's going to be some code. There might be some R code in the form of both raw and unused scripts. These are kind of things that you code up to see what's going on, perhaps in the process of making exploratory figures. There's going to be R code that you eventually don't use in the end. So, you'll have some scripts lying around. There will be some final scripts that you use in the final analysis. And these will, hopefully, be easier to read, commented and formatted better. And then you might be running some R markdown files that annotate a data analysis using a literate statistical programming style.

And finally there's going to be some text that you write, either in the form of README files that explain what's going on in your project, a more formal report that you have to write, or even a paper that you plan on publishing. All this text is going to integrate everything you've done in this data analysis, with the data, the figures, the tables, and the R code.

Raw and Processed Data

The raw data will come in any number of different forms. They might come, for example, as just records or as formatted text. You're going to do something to this raw data to make it usable for an analysis type of program. For example, you might do some text processing. You might try to parse the data and if it's formatted in a special format, you can generate something that can be later used for modeling or other types of analysis. You want to store this raw data in your analysis folder if you're working on a project. If the data were accessed from the web you want to include things like the URL, where you got the data, what the data set is, a brief description of what it's for, the date that you accessed the URL on, the website, etc. You may want this in a README file so when you look at it later, or if someone else looks at it, they know where this data came from and what it's for.

Another thing that I like to do, if you're using git or an equivalent version control system to track things that are going on in your project, is to add your data set, your raw data, if possible. If it's too big then it's not really feasible. But you can add your raw data to the repository and, in the log message, when you add it you can talk about what the website was where you got it, what the URL was, et cetera. That's a convenient place to put this kind of information.

Processed data is usually cleaner than the raw data. It can come in a variety of forms. One common format is a table. Your processed data should be named so that you can easily see what script generated what data. The processing script is very important because it shows you how the raw data were mapped to the processed data. In any README file or any sort of documentation, it's important to document what code files were used to transform the raw data into the processed data. Finally, the processed data should be tidy[18] so that you can use them in subsequent modeling or analysis types of functions.

Figures

Exploratory figures are usually very simple figures. These are figures that you make in the course of your analysis as you're getting a look at the data. Typically, your data will be high dimensional because you'll be collecting lots of variables on lots of subjects or observations. You're going to be able to look at pieces of the data at a time. **Exploratory figures serve the role of giving you a quick look at various aspects of your data.** They're not all necessarily going to be part of your final report or final paper. You'll tend to make a bunch of these along the way. They don't need to be pretty,

---

[18] http://www.jstatsoft.org/v59/i10/paper

but they need to be usable enough so that you understand what's going on in the figure and how to reproduce it. Final figures will generally be much more polished, better organized and much more readable.

The final figures usually make a very small subset of the set of exploratory figures that you might generate. For example, the typical paper in a journal might have four or maybe five figures in it because these figures take up a lot of space. You typically don't want to inundate people with a lot of figures because then the ultimate message of what you're trying to communicate tends to get lost in a pile of figures. It's important to have these final figures labeled well and annotated so people understand what's going on with the data.

Scripts

As you're doing a data analysis you'll probably burn through a lot of different R scripts and code files for various purposes. There will be a lot of dead ends that you'll go down, and there will be many R scripts that don't play into the final analysis. These R scripts are going to be less commented and contain just code that puts some stuff together. You may have multiple versions of these code files, which, typically, will include analyses that are later discarded.

Final scripts will be much more clearly commented. You'll likely have bigger comment blocks for whole sections of code. There will be a lot of small comments explaining what's going on. Any processing details of any code that is used to process the raw data would be important to include. Basically these final scripts are for any analysis that would appear in a final write up of paper.

Itâ€™s important when people see a final a product like a

paper or a report that they understand what scripts went into this report and what processing and analysis scripts might have gone into this. Then they can see the chain of events that occurred. It's important, of course, to keep a lot of the other stuff that was not used in the final report just in case someone may want to look at some of the dead ends that he went down. But that can be placed in a separate part of the project directory.

R Markdown Files

R Markdown files are also very useful (see later chapter for details). They may not be exactly required, but they can be very useful to summarize parts of an analysis or an entire analysis. R Markdown files can be used to generate *reproducible reports*. You can embed code and text into the same document and then you process the document into something readable like a webpage or a PDF file. These are very easy to create in RStudio and they can be useful as an intermediate step either between just kind of code scripts, code files, data and a polished final report.

If you don't use R markdown files you may want to have README files that explain what's going on so you or another person can get a sense of the organization of the project. They could contain step by step instructions for how the analysis is conducted, what code files are called first, what are used to process the data, what are used to fit models, and what are used to kind of generate figures and things like that.

Final Report

Finally, in the end you'll probably produce a document or report, maybe a paper or summary of all of the analysis that you did. The point of this is to tell the final story of what you generated here. Typically you'll have a title, an introduction that motivates your problem, the methods that you used to refine, the results and any measures of uncertainty, and then any conclusions that you might draw from the data analysis that you did, including any pitfalls or potential problems. The important thing is that you need to tell a coherent story, to take all the analysis that you did and kind of winnow it down into a final product that has a coherent story to it.

Don't dump

You definitely should not include every analysis that you performed through the whole process, so there may be many analysis that you did but you want to narrow it down to the important parts. That does not mean you need to delete everything that you've ever did but the summary report should not include everything. And you should always include some references for the statistical methods that you use. That way people know what you used, what software you used, and what implementation was used. This is very important for again for reproducibility by others.

Summary

That's a quick overview of how to organize your data analysis, just some basic tips because every data analysis will have its specific details. There is no best way to organize a data analysis, but there are some useful guidelines that can help you maintain the reproducibility of your work. Most analyses move in the direction of "raw" to "final" or "processed". There are raw data and processed data, exploratory plots and final plots, raw scripts and final scripts. R Markdown files can be useful for bringing all these "final" elements together.

Structure of a Data Analysis: Part 1

This chapter will talk about the basic process by which data analysis will unfold. Of course, not every data analysis is the same and not every data analysis will require the same components. But I think this will serve as a useful template for understanding what the pieces of a data analysis are and how they typically flow together. If one were to write down the steps in a data analysis, you might come up with something along these lines of the following list

- Defining the question
- Defining the ideal dataset
- Determining what data you can access
- Obtaining the data
- Cleaning the data
- Exploratory data analysis
- Statistical prediction/modeling
- Interpretation of results
- Challenging of results
- Synthesis and write up
- Creating reproducible code

There may be little things that you might want to add or delete, but most data analyses have some subset of these steps.

What we're going to talk about in this chapter, Part 1, is defining the question that you're interested in, the ideal data set, determining what data you actually can access, and obtaining and cleaning the data. In the next chapter we'll talk about the remaining topics listed here.

I think the key challenge in pretty much any data analysis was well characterized by Dan Meyer, a former high school mathematics educator. In his TED Talk he said, "Ask yourselves what problem you have ever solved, that was worth solving, where you knew all the given information in advance, where you didn't have a surplus of information and have to filter it out, or you had insufficient information and had to go find some." That's a key element of data analysis; typically, you don't have all the facts or you have too much information and you have to go through it. Much of the process of data analysis is sorting through all of this stuff. So, the first part of data analysis that you want to start with is defining a question.

The Question

Not every data analysis starts with a very specific or coherent question. But the more effort you can put into coming up with a reasonable question, the less effort you'll spend having to filter through a lot of stuff. Because **defining a question is the most powerful dimension reduction tool you can ever employ.** If you're interested in a specific variable, like height or weight, then you can remove a lot of other variables that don't really pertain to those criteria at all. But if you're interested in a different type of variable then you can remove another subset. The idea is, if you can narrow down your question as specifically as possible, you'll reduce the kind of noise that you'll have to deal with when you're going through a potentially very large data set. Now, sometimes you only want to look at a data set and see what is inside of the data set. Then you'll have to explore all kinds of things in a large data set. But if you can narrow down your interest to a specific type of question, it is extremely useful for simplifying your problem.

I encourage you to think about what type of question you're interested in answering *before* you go delving into all the details of your data set. The science, generally speaking, will determine what type of question you're interested in asking. That will lead you to the data. Which may lead you to applied statistics, which you use to analyze the data. If you get really ambitious you might want to think of some theoretical statistics that will generalize the methods that you apply to different types of data. Now, of course, there are relatively few people who can do that, and so I it would not be expected of everyone.

A key problem is if you randomly apply statistical methods to datasets to find an interesting answer you will almost certainly find something interesting, but it may not be reproducible and it may not be really meaningful. A proper data analysis has a scientific context, and at least some general question that we're trying to investigate which will narrow down the kind of dimensionality of the problem. Then we'll apply the appropriate statistical methods to the appropriate data.

Let's start with the very basic example of a question. A general question might be: can I automatically detect emails that are spam and those that are not? Of course, this is an important question if you use email and you want to know which emails you should read, that are important, and which emails are just spam. If you want to turn that into a data analysis problem there are many ways to answer the question. For example, you could hire someone to go through your email and figure out what's spam and what's not. But that's not really sustainable, and it's not particularly efficient. So, if you want to turn this into a data analysis question, you have to make the question a little bit more concrete and translate it using terms that are specific to data analysis tools.

A more concrete version of this question might be: can I use quantitative characteristics of the emails themselves to classify them as spam? Now we can start looking at emails and try to identify these quantitative characteristics that I want to develop so that I can classify them as spam. You've got a question, "How do I separate out my email so that I know what's spam and what's not?" Ultimately, you can get rid of all the spam and just read the real email.

The Ideal Dataset

The first thing you might want to think about is what is the ideal data set for this problem? If I had all the resources in the world, what would I go out to look for? There are different types of data sets that you could potentially collect depending on the goal and the type of question you're asking.

If you're interested in a descriptive problem, you might think of a whole population. You don't need to sample anything. You might want to get the entire census or population that you're looking for. So all the emails in the universe, for example. If you just want to explore your question, you might take a random sample with a bunch of variables measured.

If you want to make inference about a problem then you have to be very careful about the sampling mechanism and the definition of the population that you are sampling from. Typically, when you make an inferential statement, you use your smaller sample to make a conclusion about a larger population. Therefore, the sampling mechanism is very important. If you want to make a prediction, you need something like a training set and a test data set from a population that you're interested in so that you can build a model and a classifier.

If you want to make a causal statement, such as "if I modify this component, then something else happens," you're going to need experimental data. One type of experimental data is from something like a randomized trial or a randomized study. If you want to make mechanistic types of statements, you need data about all the different components of the system that you're trying to describe.

For our problem with spam, perhaps you use Gmail. You know that all the emails in the Gmail system are going to be stored on Google's data centers. Why don't we just get all the data (emails) in Google's data centers? That would be a whole *population* of emails. Then we can just build our classifier based on all this data and we wouldn't have to worry about sampling because we'd have all the data. That would be an example of an ideal data set.

Of course, in the real world, you have to think about what data you can actually access, right? Maybe someone at Google can actually access all the emails that go through Gmail, but even in that extreme case, it may be difficult. Furthermore, most people are not going to be able to access that. So, sometimes you have to go for something that is not quite the ideal data set. You might be able to find free data on the web. You might need to buy some data from a provider, being sure to respect the terms of use for the data. Any agreement or contract that you agree to about the data has to be adhered to. If the data simply does not exist out there, you may need to generate the data yourself in some way.

The Real Dataset

Getting all the data from Google will probably not be possible. I'm guessing their data centers have some very high security, so we're going to have to go with something else. One possible solution comes from the UCI machine learning repository, which is the spam data set. This is a collection of spam in a data set created by people at Hewlett Packard who collected several thousand spam and regular messages, then classified them appropriately. You can use this database to explore your problem of how to classify emails into spam. When you obtain the data, the first goal is to try to obtain the raw data. For example, from the UCI machine learning repository.

You have to be careful to reference the source, so wherever you get the data from, you should always reference and keep track of where it came from. If you need to get data from a person or an investigator that you're not familiar with, often a very polite email will go a long way. They may be willing to share that data with you. If you get data from an Internet source, you should always make sure at the very minimum to record the URL, which is the web site indicator of where you got the data, and the time and date that you accessed it so people have a reference of when that data was available. In the future, the website might go down or the URL may change or may not be available, but at least at the time you got that data you documented how you got it.

Cleaning the Data

The data set that we're going to talk about in this example, since we don't have access to Google's data centers, is the spam data set which you can get from the `kernlab` package in R. If you install the kernlab package, you can load the data set right away. The first thing that you typically need to do with any data set is to clean it a little bit. Raw data typically needs to be processed in some way to get it into a form where you can model it or feed it into a modeling program.

If the data is already pre-processed, it's important that you understand how it was done. Try to get some documentation about what the pre-processing was and how it was done. You have to understand kind of where the data come from, so for example if it came from a survey, you need to know how the sampling was done. Was it a convenience sample, or did the data come from an observational study, or perhaps from experiments? The source of the data is very important. You may need to reformat the data in a certain way to get it to work in a certain type of analysis. If the data set is extremely large you may want to sub-sample the data set to make it more manageable.

It is very important that anything you do to clean the data is recorded. Write down these steps in scripts or whatever is most convenient because you or someone else is going to have to reproduce these steps if they want to reproduce your findings. If you don't document all these pre-processing steps, then no one will ever be able to do it again.

Once you have cleaned the data and you have gotten a basic look at it, it is important to *determine if the data are good enough to solve your problems*. In some cases, you may determine that the data are not good enough. For example, you may not have enough data, you may not have enough variables or enough characteristics, or the sampling of the data may be inappropriate for your question. There may be all kinds of problems that occur to you as you clean the data.

If you determine the data are not good enough for your

question, then you've got to quit, try again, change the data, or try a different question. It is important to not simply push on with the data you have, just because that's all that you've got, because that can lead to inappropriate inferences or conclusions.

Here is our cleaned data set from the `kernlab` package that we're going to use for this example. It's already been cleaned for us, in the kernlab package, and I'm just showing you the first five variables here. There are many other variables in the data set but you can see that there are 4601 observations of the five variables. You can learn more about the dataset here[19], where it shows you where the data set came from and how it's processed.

```
library(kernlab)
data(spam)
str(spam[, 1:5])
```

```
'data.frame':   4601 obs. of  5 variables:
 $ make   : num  0 0.21 0.06 0 0 0 0 0 0.15 0.06 ...
 $ address: num  0.64 0.28 0 0 0 0 0 0 0 0.12 ...
 $ all    : num  0.64 0.5 0.71 0 0 0 0 0 0.46 0.77 ...
 $ num3d  : num  0 0 0 0 0 0 0 0 0 0 ...
 $ our    : num  0.32 0.14 1.23 0.63 0.63 1.85 1.92 1.8\
8 0.61 0.19 ...
```

Note if the `kernlab` package isn't installed, you can install it from CRAN using the `install.packages()` function.

---

[19] http://search.r-project.org/library/kernlab/html/spam.html

Structure of a Data Analysis: Part 2

Jumping off from the previous chapter, we can define some further steps in a data analysis to be

- Exploratory data analysis
- Statistical prediction/modeling
- Interpretation of results
- Challenging of results
- Synthesis and write up
- Creating reproducible code

Understanding each of these steps and documenting them carefully through scripts and other tools is essential for reproducibility.

In this chapter, we're going to continue the data analysis example that we started in part one. If you recall, we laid down a list of steps that generally one might take when doing a data analysis. And previously we talked about the first roughly half of these steps. In this chapter, we're going to talk about the remaining half. This includes exploratory data analysis, statistical prediction and modeling, interpretation, challenging your results, synthesizing and writing up the results, and creating reproducible code.

The basic question was, can I automatically detect emails that are SPAM or not? And a slightly more concrete version of this question that can be used to translate into a Cisco problem was, can I use quantitative characteristics of the emails to classify them as SPAM or HAM?

Splitting the Dataset

Our data set, again, was f=rom this UCI Machine Learning Repository, which had already been cleaned up, and it was available in the current lab package as a data set. This data set had 4,600 observations or emails that had been kind of characterized along 58 different variables. So, the first thing that we need to do with this data set if we want to build a model to classify emails into spam or not, is that we need to split the data set into test set and a training set. The idea is that we're going to use part of the test of the data set to build our model, and then we're going to use another part of the data set which is independent of the first part to actually determine how good our model is kind of making a prediction.

```
library(kernlab)
data(spam)

## Perform the subsampling
set.seed(3435)
trainIndicator = rbinom(4601, size = 1, prob = 0.5)
table(trainIndicator)
```

```
trainIndicator
   0    1
2314 2287
```

Here I'm a taking a random half of the data set, so I'm flipping a coin with the rbinom() function, to generate a random kind of coin flip with probability of half, so that'll separate the the data set into two pieces. You can see that roughly 2000, about 2314, are going to be in one half and

2287 will be in the other half. And so the training set will be one set and the test set will be another set of data.

```
trainSpam = spam[trainIndicator == 1, ]
testSpam = spam[trainIndicator == 0, ]
```

Exploratory Data Analysis

The first thing we're going to want to do is a little bit of exploratory data analysis. Given that we have not looked at this data set yet, it would be useful to look at what are the data, what did the data look like, what's the distribution of the data, what are the relationships between the variables. We want to look at basic summaries, one dimensional, two dimensional summaries of the data and we want to check for is there any missing data, why is there missing data, if there is, create some exploratory plots and do a little exploratory analyses.

If we look at the training data sets, that's what we're going to focus on right now as we do our exploratory analysis and as we build our model, all that's going to be done in the training data set. And if you look at the column names of the dataset, you can see that they're all just words essentially.

```
head(names(trainSpam), 20)
```

Structure of a Data Analysis: Part 2

```
 [1] "make"     "address"  "all"      "num3d"    "o\
ur"
 [6] "over"     "remove"   "internet" "order"    "m\
ail"
[11] "receive"  "will"     "people"   "report"   "a\
ddresses"
[16] "free"     "business" "email"    "you"      "c\
redit"
```

If you look at the first five rows, we can see that basically these are the frequencies at which they occur in a given email.

```
head(trainSpam[, 1:10])
```

```
   make address  all num3d  our over remove internet or\
der mail
1  0.00    0.64 0.64     0 0.32 0.00   0.00        0 0\
.00 0.00
7  0.00    0.00 0.00     0 1.92 0.00   0.00        0 0\
.00 0.64
9  0.15    0.00 0.46     0 0.61 0.00   0.30        0 0\
.92 0.76
12 0.00    0.00 0.25     0 0.38 0.25   0.25        0 0\
.00 0.00
14 0.00    0.00 0.00     0 0.90 0.00   0.90        0 0\
.00 0.90
16 0.00    0.42 0.42     0 1.27 0.00   0.42        0 0\
.00 1.27
```

You can see the word "make" does not appear in that first email and, and the word "mail" does not appear. These are all basically frequency counts, or frequencies of words within each of the emails. If we look at the training data set and look at the outcome, we see that 906 of the emails are spam, are classified as spam.

```
table(trainSpam$type)
```

```
nonspam    spam
   1381     906
```

And the other 1381 are classified as non-spam. This is what we're going to use to build our model for predicting the spam emails. We can make some plots and we can compare, what are the frequencies of certain characteristics between the spam and the non spam emails.

Here we're looking at a variable called `capitalAve`, the average number of capital letters.

```
boxplot(capitalAve ~ type, data = trainSpam)
```

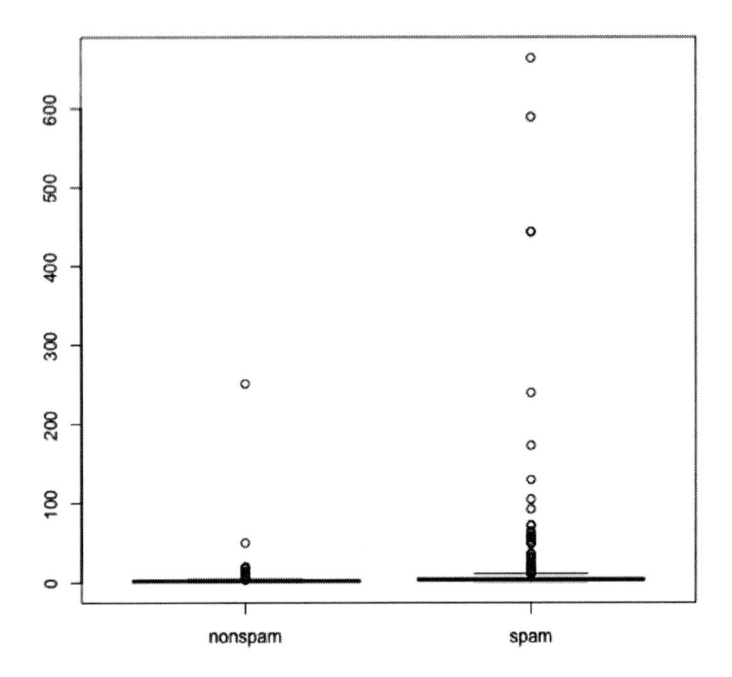

Comparison of 'capitalAve' between spam and non-spam emails

And, you can see that it's difficult to look at this picture, because the data are highly skewed. And so, in these kinds of situations it's often useful to just look at the log transformation of the variable. Here I'm going to to take the base ten log of the variable, and compare them to spam and nonspam. Since there are a lot of zeros in this particular variable, taking the log of zero doesn't really make sense. We'll just add 1 to that variable, just so we can take the log and get a rough sense of what the data look like. Typically, you wouldn't want to just add 1 to a variable just because. But since we're just exploring the data, making exploratory plots, it's okay to do that in this case.

```
boxplot(log10(capitalAve + 1) ~ type, data = trainSpam)
```

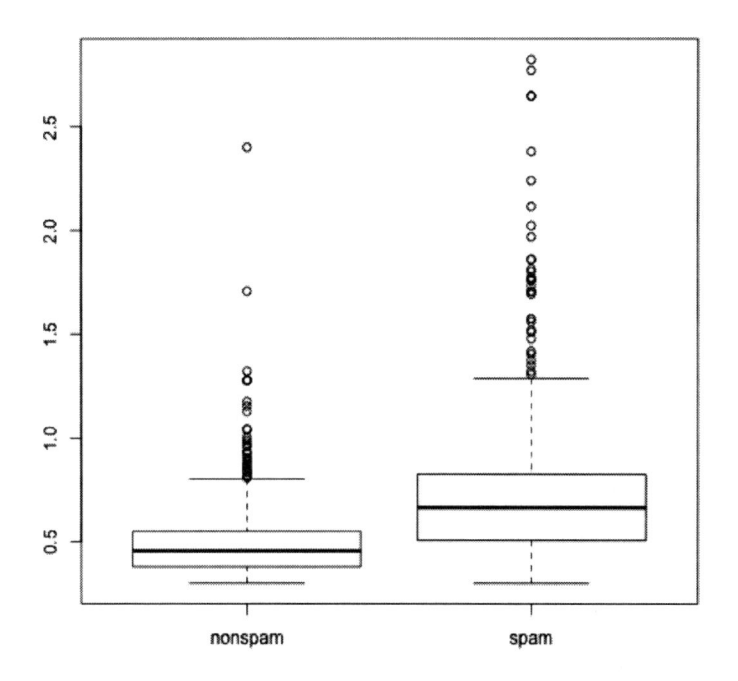

Log transformed 'captialAve'

Here you can see clearlyb that the spam emails have a much higher rate of these capital letters than the non spam emails, and of course, if you've ever seen spam emails, you're probably familiar with that phenomenon. And so that's one useful relationship to see there.

We can look at pairwise relationships between the different variables in the plots. Here I've got a pairs plot of the first four variables, and this is the log transformation of each of the variables.

```
pairs(log10(trainSpam[, 1:4] + 1))
```

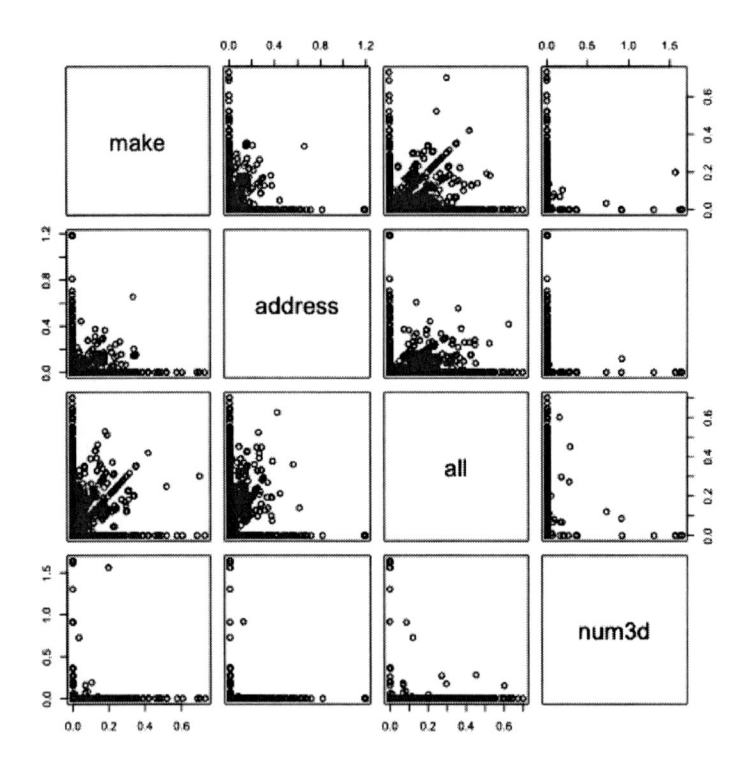

Paris plot of 4 variables

And you can see that some of them are correlated, some of them are not particularly correlated, and that's useful to know.

We can explore the predictors space a little bit more by doing a hierarchical cluster analysis, and so this is a first cut at trying to do that with the hclust function in R. I plotted the Dendrogram just to see how what predictors or what words or characteristics tend to cluster together.

```
hCluster = hclust(dist(t(trainSpam[, 1:57])))
plot(hCluster)
```

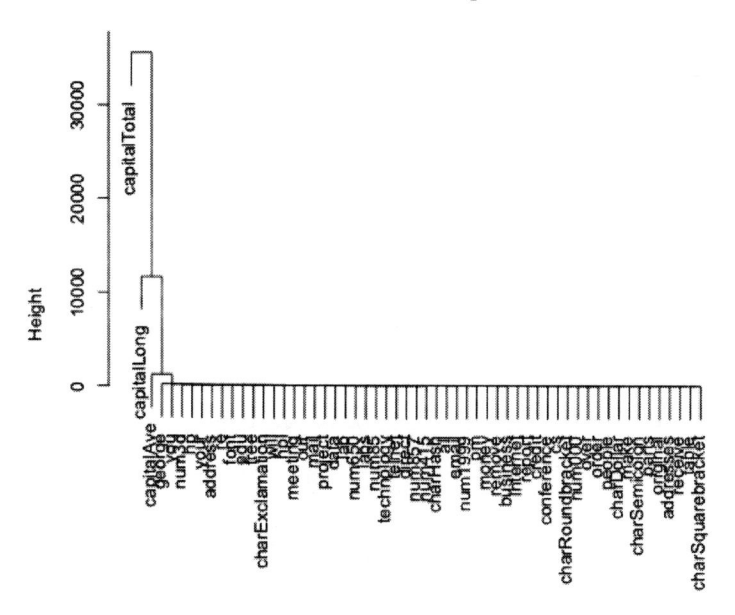

Cluster Dendrogram

dist(t(trainSpam[, 1:57]))
hclust (*, "complete")

Hierarchal cluster analysis

It's not particularly helpful at this point, although it does separate out this one variable, capital total. But if you recall, the clustering algorithms can be sensitive to any skewness in the distribution of the individual variables, so it may be useful to redo the clustering analysis after a transformation of the predictor space.

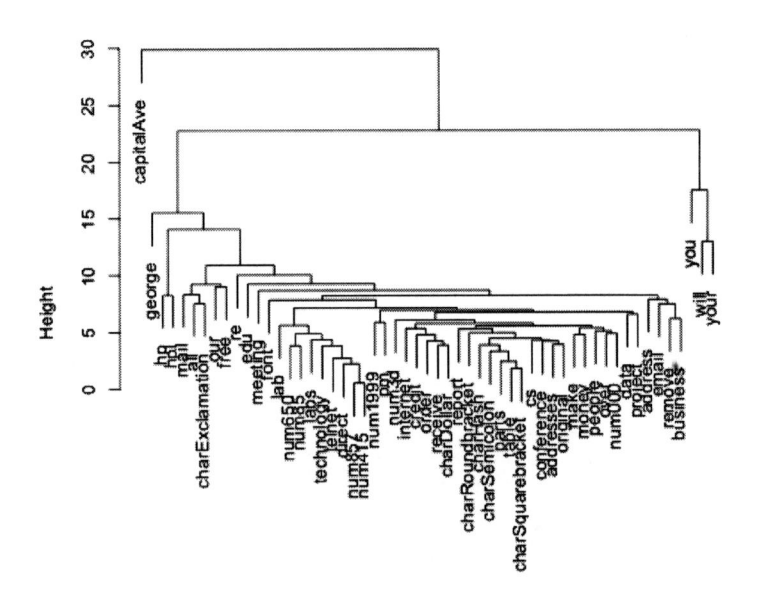

```
hClusterUpdated = hclust(dist(t(log10(trainSpam[, 1:55]\
 + 1))))
plot(hClusterUpdated)
```

Cluster Dendrogram

dist(t(log10(trainSpam[, 1:55] + 1)))
hclust (*, "complete")

Hierarchical cluster analysis of log-transformed data

Here I've taken a log transformation of the predictors in the training data set, and again, I've added one to each one, just to avoid taking the log of zero. And now you can see the dendrogram a little bit more interesting. It's separated out a few clusters and this `captialAve` is one kind of cluster all by itself. There's another cluster that includes "you will" or "your". And then there are a bunch of other words that lump more ambiguously together. And so this may be something worth exploring a little bit further, if you see some particular characteristics that are interesting.

Once we've done exploratory data analysis, we've looked at some univariate and bivariate plots, we did a little cluster analysis, we can move on to doing a more sophisticated statistical model and some prediction modeling. And so any statistical modeling that you engage in should be informed by questions that you're interested in, of course, and the results of any exploratory analysis. The exact methods that you employ will depend on the question of interest. And when you do a statistical model, you should account for the fact that the data have been processed or transformed, if they have, in fact, been so. As you do statistical modeling, you should always think about, what are the measures of uncertainty? What are the sources of uncertainty in your data set?

Statistical Modeling

Here we're going to just do a very basic statistical model. What we're going to do is we're going to go through each of the variables in the data set and try to fit a generalize linear model, in this case a logistic regression, to see if we can predict if an email is spam or not by using just a single variable.

Here, using the reformulate function to create a formula that includes the response, which is just the type of email and one of the variables of the data set, and we're just going to cycle through all the variables in this data set using this for-loop to build a logistic regression model, and then subsequently calculate the cross validated error rate of predicting spam emails from a single variable.

```
trainSpam$numType = as.numeric(trainSpam$type) - 1
costFunction = function(x, y) sum(x != (y > 0.5))
cvError = rep(NA, 55)
library(boot)
for (i in 1:55) {
    lmFormula = reformulate(names(trainSpam)[i], respon\
se = "numType")
    glmFit = glm(lmFormula, family = "binomial", data =\
 trainSpam)
    cvError[i] = cv.glm(trainSpam, glmFit, costFunction\
, 2)$delta[2]
}

## Which predictor has minimum cross-validated error?
names(trainSpam)[which.min(cvError)]
```

```
[1] "charDollar"
```

Once we've done this, we're going to try to figure out which of the individual variables has the minimum cross validated error rate. And so we can just go, and you can take this vector of results, this CV error, and just figure out which one is the minimum.

It turns out that the predictor that has the minimum cross validated error rate is this variable called charDollar. This is an indicator of the number of dollar signs in the email. Keep in mind this is a very simple model. Each of these models that we fit only have a single predictor in it. Of course we could think of something more complicated, but this may be an interesting place to start.

If we take this best model from this set of 55 predictors, this `charDollar` variable, and I'll just re-fit the model again right here. This is a logistic regression model. We can actually make predictions now from the model on the test data. Recall that we split the data set into two parts and built the training model on the training data set. Now we're going to predict the outcome on the test data set to see how well we do.

In a logistic regression we don't get specific 0/1 classifications of each of the messages, we get a probability that a message is going to be spam or not. Then we have to take this continuous probability, which ranges between 0 and 1, and determine at what point, at what cutoff, do we think that the email is spam. We're just going to draw the cut off here at 0.5, so if the probability is above 50%, we're just going to call it a spam email.

```
## Use the best model from the group
predictionModel = glm(numType ~ charDollar, family = "binomial", data = trainSpam)

## Get predictions on the test set
predictionTest = predict(predictionModel, testSpam)
predictedSpam = rep("nonspam", dim(testSpam)[1])

## Classify as 'spam' for those with prob > 0.5
predictedSpam[predictionModel$fitted > 0.5] = "spam"
```

Once we've created our classification, we can take a look at the predicted values from our model, and then compare them with the actual values from the test data set, because we know which was spam, and which was not. Here's the classification table that we get from the predicted and the the real values.

```
table(predictedSpam, testSpam$type)
```

```
predictedSpam nonspam spam
      nonspam    1346  458
      spam         61  449
```

Now we can just calculate the error rate. The mistakes that we made are on the off diagonal elements of this table, so 61 and 458. So, 61 were classified as spam that were not actually spam, and 458 were classified as non spam but actually were spam. So we calculate this error rate as about 22%.

```
## Error rate
(61 + 458)/(1346 + 458 + 61 + 449)
```

```
[1] 0.2242869
```

Interpreting Results

So far we've done the analysis, calculated some results, calculated our best model, and looked at the error rate that's produced by that model. Now we need to interpret our findings and it's important when you interpret your findings to use appropriate language and to not use language that goes beyond the analysis that you actually did. If you're in this type of application where we're just looking at some data and building a predictive model, you want to use words like, "prediction" or "it correlates with" or "certain variables may be associated with the outcome" or "the analysis is descriptive". Think carefully about what kind of language you use to interpret your results. It's also good to give an explanation for why certain models predict better than others, if possible.

If there are coefficients in the model that you need to interpret, you can do that here. And in particular it's useful to bring in measures of uncertainty, to calibrate your interpretation of the final results. In this example, we might think of stating that the fraction of characters that are dollar signs can be used to predict if an email is spam. Maybe we decide that anything with more than 6.6% dollar signs is classified as spam. More dollar signs always means more spam under our prediction model. And for our model in the test data set, the error rate was 22.4%.

Challenge the Findings

Once you've done your analysis and you've developed your interpretation, it's important that you, yourself, challenge all the results that you've found. Because if you don't do it, someone else is going to do it once they see your analysis, and so you might as well get one step ahead of everyone by doing it yourself first. It's good to challenge everything, the whole process by which you've gone through this problem. Is the question even a valid question to ask? Where did the data come from? How did you get the data? How did you process the data? How did you do the analysis and draw any conclusions?

If you have measures of uncertainty, are those the appropriate measures of uncertainty? And if you built models, why is your model the best model? Why is it an appropriate model for this problem? How do you choose the things to include in your model? All these things are questions that you should ask yourself and should have a reasonable answer to, so that when someone else asks you, you can respond in kind.

It's also useful to think of potential alternative analyses that might be useful. It doesn't mean that you have to do those alternative analyses, in the sense that you might stick to your original just because of other reasons. But it may be useful to try alternative analyses just in case they may be useful in different ways or may produce better predictions.

Synthesizing Results

Once you've interpreted your results, you've done the analysis, you've interpreted your results, you've drawn some conclusions, and you've challenged all your findings, you're going to need to synthesize the results and write them up. Synthesis is very important because typically in any data analysis, there are going to be many, many, many things that you did. And when you present them to another person or to a group you're going to want to have winnowed it down to the most important aspects to tell a coherent story. Typically you want to lead with the question that you were trying to address. If people understand the question then they can draw up a context in their mind, and have a better understanding of the framework in which you're operating. That will lead to what kinds of data are necessary, are appropriate for this question, what kinds of analyses would be appropriate.

You can summarize the analyses as you're telling the story. It's important that you don't include every analysis that you ever did, but only if its needed for telling a coherent story. It's useful to sometimes keep these analyses in your back pocket though, even if you don't talk about it, because someone may challenge what you've done and it's useful to say, "Well, you know we *did* do that analysis but it was problematic because of" whatever the reason may be.

It's usually not that useful to talk about the analyses that you did chronologically, or the order in which you did them, because the order in which you did them is often very scattered and doesn't make sense in retrospect. Talk about the analyses of your data set in the order that's appropriate for the story you're trying to tell. When you're telling the story or you're presenting to someone or to your group it's useful to include very well done figures so that people can understand what you're trying to say in one picture or two.

In our example, the basic question was "Can we use quantitative characteristics of the emails to classify them as spam or ham?" Our approach was rather than try to get the ideal data set from all Google servers, we collected some data from the UCI machine learning repository and created training and test sets from this data set. We explored some relationships between the various predictors. We decided to use a logistic regression model on the training set and chose our single variable predictor by using cross validation. When we applied this model to the test set it was 78% accurate. The interpretation of our results was that basically, more dollar signs seemed to indicate an email was more likely to be spam, and this seems reasonable. We've all seen emails with lots of dollar signs in them trying to sell you something. This is both reasonable and understandable. Of course, the results were not particularly great as 78% test set accuracy is not that good for most prediction algorithms. We probably could do much better if we included more variables or if we included a more sophisticated model, maybe a non-linear model. These are the kinds of things that you want to outline to people as you go through data analysis and present it to other people.

Reproducible Code

Finally, the thing that you want to make sure of is that you document your analysis as you go. You can use things like tools like R Markdown and knitr and RStudio to document your analyses as you do them (more about this in later chapters). You can preserve the R code as well as any kind of a written summary of your analysis in a single document using knitr. And so then to make sure that all of what you do is reproducible by either yourself or by other people, because ultimately that's the standard by which most big data analysis will be judged. If someone cannot reproduce it then the conclusions that you draw will be not as worthy as an analysis where the results are reproducible. So try to stay organized. Try to use the tools for reproducible research to keep things organized and reproducible. And that will make your evidence for your conclusions much more powerful.

Markdown

Markdown is a tool for writing for the web. In the words of its creator John Gruber[20]

> "Markdown is a text-to-HTML conversion tool for web writers. Markdown allows you to write using an easy-to-read, easy-to-write plain text format, then convert it to structurally valid XHTML (or HTML)."

Since its inception, Markdown has evolved to be widely adopted for a variety of purposes, far beyond writing for the web. In particular, the book you are reading was written in Markdown.

The name "Markdown" is a play on the names of of many "markup" languages. Its key feature is that it can be read as-is, without any special formatting. Many markup languages, like HTML or LaTeX, require that numerous formatting elements (tags) be included in the text to instruct the program that will be formatting the text for reading on how to display the text. While this gives great control over the look and feel of the text to the writer, it can greatly obscure the source text itself, making the text difficult to read and edit. With HTML, some of the tag clutter was removed with the use of cascading style sheets (CSS), but there is still quite a bit of clutter in most HTML documents.

The benefit of Markdown for writers is that it allows one to focus on writing as opposed to formatting. It has simple

---

[20] http://daringfireball.net/

and minimal yet intuitive formatting elements and can be easily converted to valid HTML (and other formats) using existing tools.

Complete information about Markdown is available at the Markdown web site[21] maintained by John Gruber. You'll notice that the web page is short. There's not much to describe! There's also some background information[22] about Markdown at Gruber's site.

What is R Markdown?

R markdown is the integration of R code with Markdown. Documents written in R Markdown have R coded nested inside of them, which allows one to to create documents containing "live" R code. R Markdown files cannot be evaluated using standard Markdown tools. Rather, R code is evaluated as part of the processing of the Markdown before the traditional Markdown tools are called.

R markdown can be converted to standard markdown using the knitr[23] package in R. Results from R code are inserted into Markdown document. Markdown can subsequently be converted to HTML using the markdown[24] package in R, but you seldom have to call this package explicitly.

The use of R Markdown to create reproducible reports is now a core tool in *literate statistical programming* and has largely replaced previous tools. The key reason for its usefulness is the simplicity of Markdown as the main documentation language, the powerful support provided by

---

[21] http://daringfireball.net/projects/markdown/
[22] http://daringfireball.net/2004/03/dive_into_markdown
[23] http://yihui.name/knitr/
[24] https://github.com/rstudio/markdown

the `knitr` package, and the integration of R Markdown into widely used products like RStudio.

One co-benefit of using R Markdown is that any basic text editor can be used to create a document. No special editing tools are needed (the editor that comes with RStudio, for example, is quite reasonable). The R Markdown to Markdown to HTML work flow can be easily managed using R Studio[25] (but is not required). Lastly, R Markdown documents have the benefit that they are purely textual documents that can play well with version control systems that are primarily designed to track changes in text files.

Markdown Syntax

Markdown has a very simple syntax that we will briefly review here.

Headings

```
# This is a primary heading (think <h1> in HTML)
## This is a secondary heading
### This is a tertiary heading
```

Italics

```
*This text will appear italicized!*
_so will this text_
```

This text will appear italicized!
so will this text

Bold

---

[25] http://rstudio.org

```
**This text will appear bold!**
__as will this text__
```

This text will appear bold!
as will this text

Unordered Lists

```
- first item in list
- second item in list
- third item in list
```

- first item in list
- second item in list
- third item in list

Ordered Lists

```
1. first item in list
2. second item in list
3. third item in list
```

1. first item in list
2. second item in list
3. third item in list

Note that you don't have to worry about the specific ordering of the *numbers* in the ordered list. As long as there are numbers there, Markdown will put them in the right order.

The following Markdown source

```
1. first item in list
2. second item in list
4. Whoops! Forgot one
3. third item in list
```

will get processed as

1. first item in list
2. second item in list
3. Whoops! Forgot one
4. third item in list

Links

Inline links can be formatted with the following syntax.

```
The number one school of the public health is the [John\
s Hopkins Bloomberg School of Public Health](http://www\
.jhsph.edu/).

The first thing you always want to do is [Download R](h\
ttp://www.r-project.org/).

The second thing you want to do is get [RStudio](http:/\
/www.rstudio.com/).
```

The number one school of the public health is the Johns Hopkins Bloomberg School of Public Health[26].

The first thing you always want to do is Download R[27].

The second thing you want to do is get RStudio[28].

---

[26] http://www.jhsph.edu/
[27] http://www.r-project.org/
[28] http://www.rstudio.com/

Occasionally, have to put so many links into a document that the document starts getting difficult to read because of all the URLs. In that case, there is an alternate approach to linking that is akin to inserting footnotes.

```
I spend so much time reading [R bloggers][1] and [Simpl\
y Statistics][2]!

[1]: http://www.r-bloggers.com/    "R bloggers"
[2]: http://simplystatistics.org/  "Simply Statistics"
```

I spend so much time reading R bloggers[29] and Simply Statistics[30]!

In the above text, the full links can be placed at the bottom of a document for convenience. The resulting formatted text is identical using both approaches, however, the source text will be easier to read because it is less cluttered.

Newlines

Newlines require a double space after the end of a line.

If you just hit "enter/return" at the end of a line this is what you get.

```
First line
Second line
```

First line Second line

However, if you put **two spaces** after the end of the first line, this is what youget.

---

[29] http://www.r-bloggers.com/
[30] http://simplystatistics.org/

```
First line
Second line
```

First line
Second line

Markdown Resources

- The Offical Markdown Documentation[31]
- Github's Markdown Guide[32]

---

[31] http://daringfireball.net/projects/markdown/basics
[32] https://help.github.com/articles/github-flavored-markdown

Using `knitr` for Reproducible Reports

There are a number of challenges to making reproducible report writing a reality. Authors must undertake considerable effort to put data and results on the web or at least to make them available to a wide audience. Readers must download those data and results individually and piece together which data go with which code sections. Often both authors and readers must manually interact with websites, in a highly non-automated process. Finally, there is often no single document to integrate data analysis with textual representations, so the data, code, and text are not linked together in a coherent manner.

A general solution that attempts to address some of these challenges is literate statistical programming, a concept we introduced earlier in this book. For those of you who are skipping around, the idea of literate programming comes from Donald Knuth, who envisioned computer code and the documentation for that code existing together in a single document.

For literate *statistical* programming, the idea is that a report is viewed as a stream of text and code. Analysis code is divided into code chunks with text surrounding the code chunks explaining what is going on. In general, literate programs are *weaved* to produce human-readable documents and *tangled* to produce machine- readable documents

The requirements for writing literate programs are a **documentation language** and a **programming language**. Knuth's original WEB system used TeX as the documentation language and Pascal as the programming language. Fritz Leisch originally developed the Sweave system for R, which used LaTeX as the documentation language and R as the programming language. This system was very powerful, and quite useful for those mathematically and statistically inclined users for whom LaTeX was a commonly used markup language. However, the requirement to learn LaTeX was a high barrier for mamy people, higher even than learning R, if only because people saw few benefits to learning LaTeX except to use a system like Sweave. Sweave still comes with every R installation and is maintained by the R Core members.

Literate Statistical Programming: Pros and Cons

Before we go on to the details of using `knitr` for reproducible reports, we should note that there are both advantages and disadvantages to using a literate programming system for writing reports. Some of the advantages are that

- Text and code are all in one place and placed in a logical order as dictated by the flow of the data analysis
- Results are automatically updated to reflect external changes to data, code, etc.
- Code is live; this helps to serve as a built in regression test when building a document—if you can't run the code, you can't build the document.

On the other hand, there are some disadvantages:

- Text and code all in one place! This can sometimes make documents difficult to read, especially if there

is *a lot* of code. It might make sense to place code in a separate file, but they you are introducing more complexity and more chances for non-reproducibility.
- The processing of documents can be very slow, especially if the document is long. However, there are now tools that can help with that (somewhat). In general, literate statistical programming tools are awkward to use for very long or very complex documents. In those cases, it's better to use literate programming tools in conjunction with other tools, like Makefiles.

My general feeling is that knitr is ideal for

- Manuals
- Short/medium-length technical documents
- Tutorials
- Reports, especially if they will be generated periodically with updated data
- Data preprocessing documents and summaries

I feel that knitr is NOT particularly well-suited for the following:

- Very long research articles
- Documenting very complex and time-consuming computations
- Documents that require precise formatting (although this is more an issue with using Markdown than it is with using knitr)

The `knitr` Packages

The `knitr` package was developed by Yihui Xie[33], while he was a graduate student at Iowa State University. The `knitr` package many of the ideas that had been developed in separate packages since the introduction of Sweave and combined them all together into one logical package/framework. The package supports a variety of documentation languages (Markdown, LaTeX, and HTML) and a variety of programming languages. The package also supports weaving to PDF and HTML formats (in RStudio you can also weave to Microsoft Word docx format). For the purposes of this book, we will focus on using Markdown as the documentation language and R as the programming language and assume you are exporting to HTML format.

The `knitr` package is available from your local CRAN mirror and can be installed with the `install.packages()` function in R. One key feature of the RStudio IDE (among many) is that `knitr` is built right into the GUI so that you can write documents with `knitr` without having to write at the console.

To use the `knitr` package, you need

- A recent version of R
- A text editor for writing R Markdown documents (the one that comes with RStudio is fine)
- Some support packages installed (also available on CRAN)
- Some knowledge of Markdown, LaTeX, or HTML

As noted above, we will focus on using Markdown here.

---

[33] http://yihui.name

My First `knitr` Document

Here's an example of creating a simple R Markdown document in RStudio. To create a new document, you can click on the menu in the upper left hand side of the GUI.

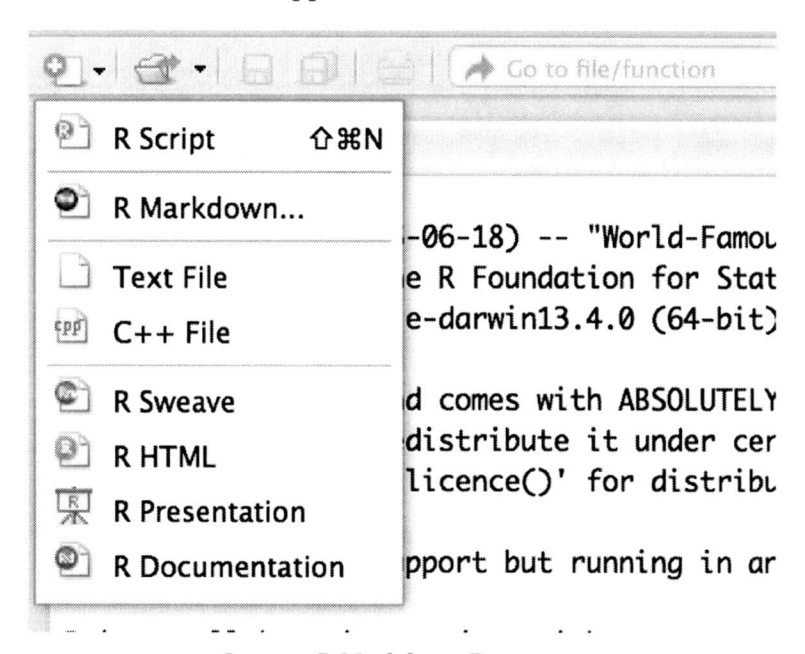

Open an R Markdown Document

RStudio will prompt you with a dialog box to set some of the metadata for the document. You can feel free to either fill this out now or just click OK. Either way, you can always make changes to this information later.

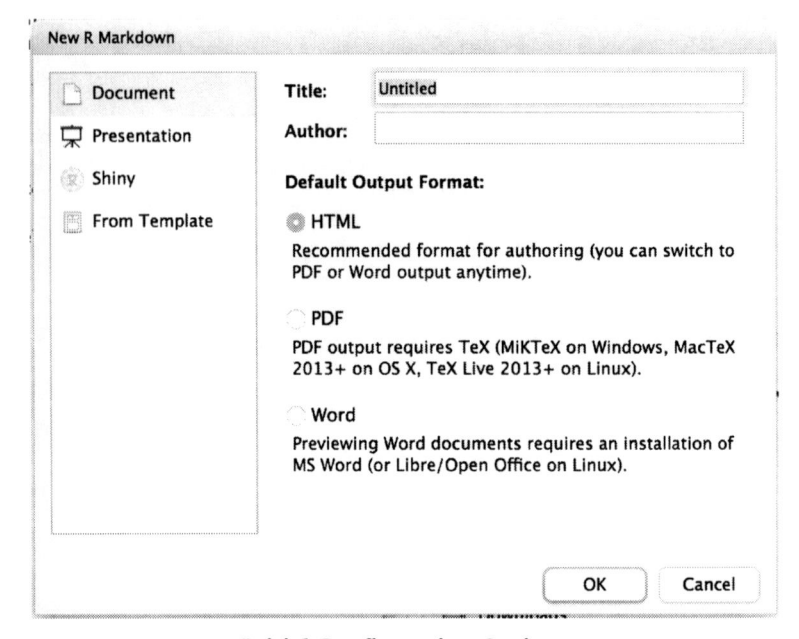

Initial Configuration Options

Initially, RStudio creates the R Markdown document with some filler text. Don't worry about this text, you can feel free to delete later it when you're ready to write your document. However, if you're new to R Markdown, you might want to take a look at it to get a feel of how R Markdown documents are written.

```
 1  ---
 2  title: "Untitled"
 3  output: html_document
 4  ---
 5
 6  This is an R Markdown document. Markdown is a simple formatting syntax f
    authoring HTML, PDF, and MS Word documents. For more details on using R
    see <http://rmarkdown.rstudio.com>.
 7
 8  When you click the **Knit** button a document will be generated that inc
    content as well as the output of any embedded R code chunks within the d
    You can embed an R code chunk like this:
 9
10  ```{r}
11  summary(cars)
12  ```
13
```

Initial Document with Boilerplate Text

Processing an R Markdown Document

When you are ready to process and view your R Markdown document the easiest thing to do is click on the `Knit HTML` button that appears at the top of the editor window. For now, just leave the boiler

```
 1   ---
 2   title: "Untitled"
 3   output: html_document
 4   ---
 5
 6   This is an R Markdown document. Markdown
     authoring HTML, PDF, and MS Word documen
     see <http://rmarkdown.rstudio.com>.
```

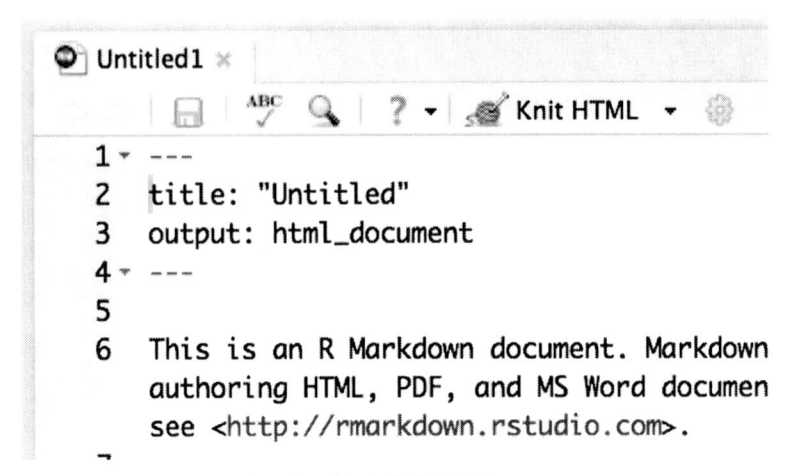

Use the "Knit HTML" Button

If you're not using RStudio, you can still process R Markdown documents with the `knitr` package directly. Assuming your R Markdown document is in your current working directory (as determined by `getwd()`) you can run

```
library(knitr)
knit2html("document.Rmd")
browseURL("document.html")
```

where `document.Rmd` and `document.html` should be substituted with whatever your file name happens to be.

HTML Output

When you click the `Knit HTML` button (or run the `knit2html()` function) the result you get should look something like this.

My First knitr Document

This is some text (i.e. a "text chunk")

Here is a code chunk

```
set.seed(1)
x <- rnorm(100)
mean(x)
```

```
## [1] 0.1088874
```

Initial HTML Output

Note here that the the code is echoed in the document in a grey background box and the output is shown just below it in a white background box. This is the default theme for the output in RStudio. For better or for worse, knitr produces (by default) a standalone HTML document with the styling information built in to the document.

Notice also that the output is prepended with two pound symbols. This is there so that if you happen to be copying code from the HTML output and pasting it into the R console, you just copy and paste the code and don't accidently paste the output too (the output will be commented out in the R console). You can turn this behavior off by setting

```
knitr::opts_chunk$set(comment = NA)
```

at the top of your document somewhere (see below for setting global options).

A Few Notes

There are a couple of things worth noting at this point. First, as you already saw, opening a new R Markdown document in RStudio will fill a new document with filler text. Just delete the filler; it's just there to demonstrate the basics of R Markdown documents.

Code chunks begin with ```` ``` ````{r} and end with just ```` ``` ````. Any R code that you include in a document must be contained within these delimiters, unless you have inline code. Code chunks can have names, which is useful when we start incorporating graphics (graphics file names are based on the code chunk name). Finally, by default, code in a code chunk is echoed back out to the document, as will the results of the computation (if there are results to print).

When you process a knitr document here's what happens under the hood:

1. You write the RMarkdown document (with a .Rmd extension)
2. knitr produces a Markdown document (with a .md extension)
3. knitr converts the Markdown document into HTML (by default)

The process is .Rmd to .md to .html; in principle there should be three documents when the process is complete, but RStudio deletes the intermediary .md file by default (you can turn this behavior off if you need the .md file)

You should NOT edit (or even save) the .md or .html documents until you are finished; these documents will be overwritten the next time you knit the .Rmd file.

Another Example

Here's an example of an R Markdown document where we modify some of the chunk-level arguments to override the defaults. In this case, we choose to NOT echo the code in the resulting document. This sometimes useful if there's just too much code and you don't want to overwhelm the reader with a print out of the code.

```
# My First knitr Document
Roger D. Peng

## Introduction

This is some text (i.e. a "text chunk")

Here is a code chunk

```{r simulation, echo=FALSE}
set.seed(1)
x <- rnorm(100)
mean(x)
```
```

Another R Markdown Example

And here is the output.

My First knitr Document

Roger D. Peng

Introduction

This is some text (i.e. a "text chunk").

Here is a code chunk

```
## [1] 0.1088874
```

Hiding Source Code

Notice that now the code is no longer in the document.

Hiding Results

In addition to hiding the code, you can hide the results of computation. This is sometimes useful if you are, for example, making a plot and you want the reader to see the final plot, not the various results of the computations that came before it. Setting the option `results = "hide"` achieves this.

```
# My First knitr Document
Roger D. Peng

## Introduction

This is some text (i.e. a "text chunk")

Here is a code chunk

```{r simulation, echo=FALSE, results="hide"}
set.seed(1)
x <- rnorm(100)
mean(x)
```
```

Hiding Results

The following output now hides both the code and the results of the code.

My First knitr Document

Roger D. Peng

Introduction

This is some text (i.e. a "text chunk")

Here is a code chunk

Output With Hiding Results

Inline Computations

Occasionally, it's useful to put some computations within a sentence. For example, you may be quoting a specific numerical results in the middle of a paragraph. Rather than try to copy and paste the result into the paragraph, it's better to just do the computation right there in the text.

In this example I'm quoting the current time and generating a random Normal variate as my "favorite" number.

```
# My First knitr Document
Roger D. Peng

## Introduction

```{r computetime, echo=FALSE}
time <- format(Sys.time(), "%a %b %d %X %Y")
```

The current time is `r time`. My favorite random number is `r rnorm(1)`.
```

Inline Computation

Here is the output from the above source. Notice that the current time is inserted into the text, as well as a random number.

My First knitr Document

Roger D. Peng

Introduction

The current time is Sat Aug 08 17:36:34 2015. My favorite random number is -0.2459739.

Inline Computation Output

Incorporating Graphics

No report of a data analysis would be complete without some sort of graphic or plot, right? Of course, incorporating data graphics with `knitr` is straightforward. By default, nothing special needs to be done. You can just put the plotting code in a code chunk and the plot will be inserted into the resulting HTML document.

```
# My First knitr Document
Roger D. Peng

## Introduction

```{r simulatedata, echo=TRUE}
set.seed(2)
x <- rnorm(100)
y <- x + rnorm(100, sd = 0.5)
```

Here is scatterplot of the data.

```{r scatterplot, fig.height=4}
par(mar = c(5, 4, 1, 1), las = 1)
plot(x, y, main = "My Simulated Data")
```
```

Creating Plots

In the example above, I decided to change the figure height to make it a bit shorter than the default. You can change the width of the plot with the `fig.width` argument in the code chunk.

When knitr creates the HTML document, by default, it embeds the figure into the HTML document as base 64 encoded string. You can see that here in the HTML below.

```
<div id="my-first-knitr-document" class="section level1">
<h1>My First knitr Document</h1>
<p>Roger D. Peng</p>
<div id="introduction" class="section level2">
<h2>Introduction</h2>
<pre class="r"><code>set.seed(2)
x &lt;- rnorm(100)
y &lt;- x + rnorm(100, sd = 0.5)</code></pre>
<p>Here is scatterplot of the data.</p>
<pre class="r"><code>par(mar = c(5, 4, 1, 1), las = 1)
plot(x, y, main = &quot;My Simulated Data&quot;)</code></pre>
<p><img
src="data:image/png;base64,iVBORw0KGgoAAAANSUhEUgAABUAAAAMACAY
I2NVd1v21QUP4lvXKQWP6Cxjg4Vi69VU1u5GxqtxgZJk6XpQhq5zdgqpMl1bhp
ElTQRXVJKQ9dNpAaJP2gqpwrq9Tu13GuJGvfznndz7v0TVAx1ea45hJGWDe8l0
sNfIcHeNwfa6/9zdVappwMknkJsVz19HvFpgJSp064PIN5G+fAp30Hc8TziHS4
zH5bAzzHIK1I08t6hq6zHpRdu2aYdJYuk9Q/881bzZa8Xrx6fLmJo/iu4/VXnf
Zp7pML5yTcW61PvIN6JuGr4halQvmjNlCa4bXJ5zj6qhpxrujeKPYMXEd+g00K
3Df08bLiHsQf+ja6gTPWVimZl7l/oUrjl8OcxDWLbNU5D6JRL2gxkDu16fGuC0
```

Generated HTML

This is useful sometimes because it makes the resulting HTML document stand alone. You can email it to a colleague and they will be able to view it without having to worry about any external dependencies like image files. However, it does make the resulting HTML much larger than it needs to be (and make sit totally unreadable). That said, given that the HTML is not meant to be read directly and is just auto-generated by knitr, it's not clear that there are many downsides to this approach.

Here's the actual output that gets rendered in the HTML viewer (or web browser).

My First knitr Document

Roger D. Peng

Introduction

```
set.seed(2)
x <- rnorm(100)
y <- x + rnorm(100, sd = 0.5)
```

Here is scatterplot of the data.

```
par(mar = c(5, 4, 1, 1), las = 1)
plot(x, y, main = "My Simulated Data")
```

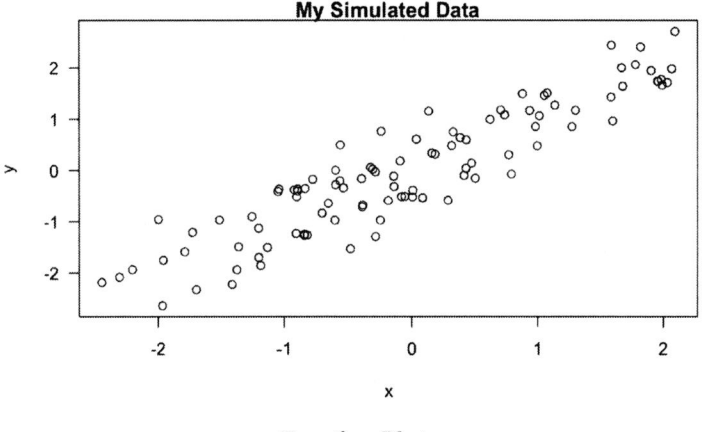

Creating Plots

Making Tables With `xtable`

Tables can be made in R Markdown documents with the help of the xtable package. Tables can be notoriously non-reproducible if they are made by hand. Luckly, the xtable package can take tabular information and format it nicely in either HTML or LaTeX. Here, we will create HTML tables.

In the code below, we fit a multiple linear regression model and then create a table of the regression coefficients. Essentially, this is the output that is generated by the `summary()` function when called on `lm` objects.

```
## Introduction

```{r fitmodel}
fit <- lm(Ozone ~ Wind + Temp + Solar.R, data = airquality)
```

Here is a table of regression coefficients.

```{r showtable, results="asis"}
library(xtable)
xt <- xtable(summary(fit))
print(xt, type = "html")
```
```

Making Tables with xtable

Notice that in the chunk options I specify `results="asis"`. This is because `xtable` generates its own HTML output, so it doesn't have to be subsequently converted into HTML by `knitr`.

The output document is below.

Introduction

```
fit <- lm(Ozone ~ Wind + Temp + Solar.R, data = airquality)
```

Here is a table of regression coefficients.

```
library(xtable)
xt <- xtable(summary(fit))
print(xt, type = "html")
```

	Estimate	Std. Error	t value	Pr(>|t|)
(Intercept)	-64.3421	23.0547	-2.79	0.0062
Wind	-3.3336	0.6544	-5.09	0.0000
Temp	1.6521	0.2535	6.52	0.0000
Solar.R	0.0598	0.0232	2.58	0.0112

Table Output from xtable

This is just one simple example of how `xtable` can be used to generate HTML tables. There are many other options that can be configured in the `print()` method for `xtable` objects and the help page is worth exploring.

Setting Global Options

Sometimes you want to set an option that applies to all chunks in your document. This can be done by modifying the `opts_chunk` variable in `knitr`, which is a global variable in the `knitr` package. Usually, this is done by creating a code chunk somewhere in the beginning of the document (before any other code chunks in the document) and modifying the `opts_chunk` object.

For example, if we wanted the default to be that all chunks do NOT echo their code and always hide their results, we could set

```
knitr::opts_chunk$set(echo = FALSE, results = "hide")
```

Any other valid chunk options can be set in the embedded `set()` function in the `opts_chunk` object.

Global options can always be overridden by any specific options that are set in at the chunk level. For example, when using the `xtable` package, I want to override the default `results` argument.

```
## Introduction

```{r setoptions, echo=FALSE}
knitr::opts_chunk$set(echo = FALSE, results = "hide")
```

First fit a linear regression model.

```{r fitmodel, echo=TRUE}
## This chunk will be displayed
fit <- lm(Ozone ~ Wind + Temp + Solar.R, data = airquality)
```

Here is a table of regression coefficients.

```{r showtable, results="asis"}
## This chunk will be hidden
library(xtable)
xt <- xtable(summary(fit))
print(xt, type = "html")
```
```

Setting Global Options

Here is the corresponding output.

Introduction

First fit a linear regression model.

```
## This chunk will be displayed
fit <- lm(Ozone ~ Wind + Temp + Solar.R, data = airquality)
```

Here is a table of regression coefficients.

	Estimate	Std. Error	t value	Pr(>|t|)
(Intercept)	-64.3421	23.0547	-2.79	0.0062
Wind	-3.3336	0.6544	-5.09	0.0000
Temp	1.6521	0.2535	6.52	0.0000
Solar.R	0.0598	0.0232	2.58	0.0112

Global Options

Caching Computations

Earlier in this chapter, I mentioned that knitr is perhaps not so useful if you are writing a very long document or one involving complex computations. However, there is one tool that can be useful and may help you circumvent some of these problems.

The basic issue is that if you have a long document or one involving lengthy computations, then every time you want to view your document in the pretty formatted version, you need to re-compile the document, meaning you need to re-run all the computations. If your code chunks are quick and not too numerous, the having to knit the document every time is not such a burden. But otherwise, it can be painful to have to sit there and wait for every computation to run every single time.

Chunk caching is one way to avoid these lengthy computations. By setting the cache = TRUE chunk option, what knitr does is run the chunk *once*, then store the output in a database in your working directory. Then, when you re-knit the document, instead of running the code in that particular chunk, knitr simply re-loads the stored output from the database. It's kind of like a chunk-level version of memoization. However, if the code in the chunk changes at all, knitr can detect this and will re-run the code (and store the reuslts again).

There some caveats to caching. In particular, by default dependencies between chunks are not checked. If the results of a cached chunk depend on a previous chunk that has been modified, those changes will not necessarily propogate down to later cached chunks. Also, chunks with significant side effects, such as those writing output to files or interacting with the external environment in any way, may not be cacheable.

Summary

Literate statistical programming can be a useful way to put text, code, data, and output all in one document. Doing this with R and Markdown, in conjuncdtion with the knitr package and RStudio, is an very easy and yet powerful tool for integrating code and text in a simple document format.

Communicating Results Over E-mail

A substantial and important part of any good data analysis involves communicating the results to others. While communication may involve writing a report, publishing a paper, or making an oral presentation, in many settings the initial "presentation" is through e-mail or something similar. In those cases, itâ€™s often useful to structure the presentation as a hierarchy, with key high-level information up front and supporting details or evidence in the background. This chapter talks about ways in which you can organize presentations so that various types of people (e.g. managers, colleagues) can extract as much useful information out as possible.

This chapter is not so much about reproducibility *per se*. It's more about how you can communicate your results in a way that people can understand them and can check or challenge your results, if they need to. Particularly, when you're working on a large data analysis, or a complex project, and you do your work in a reproducible manner, you're going to generate a lot of content, files, output, and data. These outputs cannot all be presented at once without any structure.

When you present your findings to another person there's a hierarchy of information that you're going to want to present, ranging from the least specific to most specific. The bottom line is that most people these days are very busy[34].

---

[34]http://simplystatistics.org/2011/09/23/getting-email-responses-from-busy-people/

People like managers and organization leaders are going to be *very* busy, so they are more likely to accept and digest content that you present in a streamlined and hierarchical order.

Many times when you present a data analysis, it will be in an oral form like a presentation or in a meeting. Often the early results or intermediate results are presented via a medium like e-mail. It's useful to break down the results of an analysis into different levels of specificity or granularity. The basic idea is that you don't want to blast a ton of information to someone in one go, because it'll be overwhelming and people will be less likely to read what you have to say.

Hierarchy of a Research Paper

If you think about what a typical research paper might look like, it's a hierarchy of information built into a research paper.

1. **Title and Author list**: Typically the first level is going to be the title, which is descriptive of what the paper's about. Hopefully it's interesting, it tells you a little bit about what's going on, but there's really no detail in a title, just the the topic that's covered. Also, we can learn *who* is responsible for the work from the author list.
2. **Abstract**: The next will be the abstract, usually a couple hundred words, describing what the paper's about, what motivated the problem and what was done to solve the problem.
3. **Body and Results**: Then, of course, you have the paper itself. The body of the paper will have the methods and more details about what you really did. The more

detailed results will include any sensitivity analyses and a much longer discussion of the implications of the results.
4. **Supplementary materials (gory details)**: Of course, even the written paper, for a complex data analysis, doesn't specify all the details that are needed to reproduce the findings. Typically, you might have some supplementary materials which have a lot more of the details about what was done.
5. **Code and data (*really* gory details)**: If you really want to do what was done to a level of precision that is useful, you probably need to get the code, the data and all the gory details of what happened.

That's the range of things that you might be able to present from least specific to most specific in a typical research paper.

Hierarchy of an E-mail

Not everyone is writing a research paper, but there is an analog: e-mail. If you're going to be e-mailing results either a colleague or a manager, then it's a good idea to follow a basic structure:

1. **Subject Line and Sender Information**: First line of information is the subject of the e-mail, which becomes like the title. It should be concise, you want to be descriptive, and at a minimum, you want to have one. So don't send an e-mail without a subject, it's not specific as to what the e-mail is about. If you can summarize what you've done in one sentence, it may be useful put that in the subject. That way people

reading the subject can get a sense of what's happening and maybe even make a decision based on that alone.

2. **E-mail Body**: The next level of information is the e-mail body. Even though there's no technical limit on the size of the e-mail body, you don't want to go too crazy with this. You need to provide a brief description of the problem, because the person, if they're working on many different things at once, may not remember what the problem is or precisely what you're working on. Give them a little context, give them a little description. Recall if there was a dsicussion previously. Talk about what was proposed and what you actually did. Summarize some of your findings and your results for one to two paragraphs within the e-mail body. If you need the person to take some sort of action based on the results of this presentation, try to suggest some options that and make them as concrete as possible. If there are questions that need to be addressed, it's best to make them yes/no questions, or as simple as possible.

3. **Attachments**: After the e-mail body you might attach something that's quite a bit longer, a PDF file or another type of document. This can be a report containing more detailed analyses, figures, tables, things like that. This can be derived from an R markdown file. You can use something you create with `knitr`. Even in the report like this where you may be allowed acouple of pages to present things, you still want to stay concise, you don't want to spit out pages and pages of code and tables and results. We know that your code is available because if you use something like `knitr` then obviously, you have to put the code in with the results, but you don't necessarily have to present it all in the report.

4. **Supplementary Materials**: If someone really wants to look at what you did precisely, you can give them a link to a repository, like GitHub, a project website that would have all of the details, or all your code files, all your data sets, your software environment, things like that. Those are the different levels of detail that you might want to present to someone.

There may be many different kinds of people with different levels of interest in your work who are reading the e-mail you send out. People who are truly interested in everything that you did or really want to know the details, they might go to your GitHub repository and start pulling your code and start looking at the detailed results. Conversely, someone who wants top line summaries will read the e-mail, look at the subject, read the brief description, and maybe flip through the report.

You want to present people with these different levels of detail so they can choose the level that they are most interested in. This is just a generic template for how you might present an analysis or a data, or a project that you've worked on. Not every presentation will need all these different levels but I find this to be a useful breakdown of the different types of presentations that you can make.

Reproducibility Check List

Reproducibility can be more or less easy to achieve depending on the context, the scientific area, the complexity of a data analysis, and a variety of other factors. However, over time, I've developed a few rules of thumb that I think are useful for at least encouraging reproducibility, if not guaranteeing it. In this chapter, I put together a simple "check list" of ideas that I've developed in my experience doing data analysis and computational research.

Start With Good Science

Good science, generally speaking, or a good *question*, is the key to any worthwhile investigation. The general rule of "garbage in, garbage out" applies here. If you do not start with a meaningful question, then no amount of data analysis or statistical machinery will be able to make the results interesting to you. If the question and the results are not interesting to you or your colleagues, there will be relatively little motivation to make the results reproducible. This is a problem.

Having a coherent, focused question simplifies many problems and will make it easier to determine whether you are on the right track or if an error has occurred. Vague and broadly defined questions can fit many different scenarios and are more likely to encourage sloppiness and unclear thinking.

Related to working on a problem that interests you is working with good collaborators. Collaborators that you work well with will reinforce good practices and will encourage you to do the best work. Ultimately, if you are uncomfortable with the people you are working with, or more seriously, if you do not completely *trust* the people you are working with, then there will be breakdowns in communication and things will get lost. If you don't feel comfortable (politely) challenging a colleague's work when needed, then bad work will make it through, which can lead to non-reproducible results. Working with the right people is an important, but often unmentioned, aspect of making work reproducible.

Don't Do Things By Hand

If this chapter could be boiled down to one rule, it might be "Don't do things by hand". What do I mean by that? Here are a few examples that are common, but are bad practice:

- Editing spreadsheets of data to "clean it up". Often this is doen to remove outliers, do quality assurance or quality control checks (QA/QC), or validating individual data entries
- Editing tables or figures (e.g. rounding, formatting) to make then look better
- Downloading data from a web site using a web browser
- Moving data around your computer
- Splitting or reformatting data files

Often, the motivation for doing all of the above things is that "We're just going to do this once." The thinking is that if the activity is only going to be done once, it doesn't need to be automated (i.e. programmed into a computer).

But programming a procedure into a computer is not necessarily about automation. It is also about *documentation*. The problem with things that are done by hand, is that things done by hand need to be precisely documented (this is harder than it sounds). Often, it can very difficult to communicate to someone what was done after the fact. It can be easy to miss a step that "isn't important" when in fact it is.

Don't Point And Click

Pointing and clicking is obviously related to doing things by hand. Most modern operating systems have a windowing interface that allow you to click on menus that can lead to automated built-in routines. Many data processing and statistical analysis packages have graphical user interfaces (GUIs) that simplify the use of the program, but the actions you take with a GUI can be difficult for others to reproduce because there's not necessarily a log of what was clicked.

Some GUIs for statistical analysis packages produce a log file or script which includes equivalent commands for reproducing the behavior of the GUI, but this is by no means the standard. In general, be careful with data analysis software that is highly *interactive*. There is often a trade-off between the ease of use of a software package and the tendency to lead to non-reproducible results.

Of course, this doesn't mean that all interactive software. Some software has to be interactive, like text editors or word processors, and that's fine. It's just when the software must be used to *conduct data analysis*, you must be careful not to be seduced by the ease-of-use of an interactive interface.

Teach a Computer

The opposite of doing things by hand is teaching a computer to do something. Computers need very precise instructions to accomplish a task so there's no room for ambiguity. This is a Good Thing if your goal is to make your procedures and processes reproducible. If something needs to be done as part of your analysis or investigation, try to teach your computer to do it, *even if you only need to do it once*. In the end, teaching a computer to do something almost guarantees reproducibilty.

Example: Downloading data

Downloadling datasets is something data scientists are constantly doing. But if you're using a web browser to download data, you're probably not downloading data in a reproducible way. Suppose you wanted to obtain a dataset to analyze from the UCI Machine Learning Repository. One way to do that by hand would be to

1. Go to the UCI Machine Learning Repository at http://archive.ics.
2. Download the Bike Sharing Dataset[35] by clicking on the link to the Data Folder, then clicking on the link to the zip file of dataset, and choosing "Save Linked File As..." and then saving it to a folder on your computer

But this involves doing things by hand! Normally, the interactive nature of the web browser is a great feature, but *not* when you need to download a dataset that is important to your analysis

Another way to accomplish this task is to teach your computer to do the same thing using R:

---

[35] http://archive.ics.uci.edu/ml/datasets/Bike+Sharing+Dataset

```
> download.file("http://archive.ics.uci.edu/ml/machine-\
learning-databases/00275/Bike-Sharing-Dataset.zip",
+      "ProjectData/Bike-Sharing-Dataset.zip")
```

Notice here that

- The full URL to the dataset file is specified (no clicking through a series of links)
- The name of the file saved to your local computer is specified ("Bike-Sharing-Dataset.zip")
- The directory in which the file was saved is specified ("ProjectData")
- The code can always be executed in R (as long as link is available)

Now that you've taught a computer to do this task, it is far more reproducible than writing down a series of instructions directing someone to use a web browser. In fact, the R code is a far more compact representation of this task.

Use Some Version Control

Version control systems is not something we've explicitly covered in this book so far, so I won't go into great detail here. Briefly, version control systems are software systems designed to help you keep track of changes to a set of code files in a given project. They are primarily designed for software projects where code files are typically reasonably small text files, but they can also be applied to data analysis projects. Examples of popular version control systems these days are git[36], subversion[37] (svn), and mercurial[38] (hg).

---

[36] http://git-scm.com
[37] http://subversion.apache.org
[38] https://mercurial.selenic.com

If there's one reason for using a version control system to track the changes to your data analysis project, it is that the version control system can help to **slow things down**. In many instances with data analyses, it's tempting to zoom ahead and start plowing into the data to find something interesting. This excitement is good, of course, but not at the expense of keeping track of what's happening. Version control systems can be helpful for reminding you that changes need to be tracked and notes need to be taken, if only to remind *yourself* of what happened a little be later (much less for communicating to team members).

Version control systems have many benefits, such as being able to track snapshots of a project and to mark/tag major milestones. They also allow for simple collaboration across networks (internal or external) and for publishing your work. With complementary web sites like GitHub[39], BitBucket[40], and SourceForge[41], it is now straightforward to publish your projects so that anyone can view your work. Most of these sites have some free tier that allows you to host your projects without any cost to you.

Keep Track of Your Software Environment

If you work on a complex project involving many tools and datasets, the software and computing environment can play a critical role in determining whether your analysis is reproducible. In the extreme case, if your analysis depends on some custom proprietary software or hardware that only you possess, then obviously no one else will be able

---

[39] https://github.com
[40] https://bitbucket.org
[41] http://sourceforge.net

to reproduce your analysis. However, there are many cases short of that extreme one where the software and hardware environment in which a data analysis was conducted can be important for reproducibility.

Here are a few things that you should keep in mind as you keep track of your environment.

- **Computer architecture**: What kind of CPU does your computer use? Intel, AMD, ARM, etc.? And are you using graphical processing units (GPUs)?
- **Operating system**: Are you using Windows, Mac OS, Linux / Unix, something else? The more obscure your operating system, the more difficult it might be to reproduce your work unless you do things in a cross-platform manner.
- **Software toolchain**: This includes things like compilers, interpreters, the command shell, programming languages (C, Perl, Python, etc.), database backends, and any data analysis software.
- **Supporting software and infrastructure**: Software libraries, R packages, software dependencies
- **External dependencies**: Your data analysis is likely to depend on things outside of your computer, like web sites, data repositories, remote databases, and software repositories.
- **Version numbers**: Ideally, you should keep track of the version numbers for everything you use, if possible. This is particularly important for software and libraries because often certain versions of software do not work with other versions of software, so a mismatch in version numbers may prevent another person from reproducible your work. Communicating the appropriate version numbers to others can

improve the chances of them reproducing what you've done.

One important function in R that can be useful for documenting your R environment is the `sessionInfo()` function. This function displays various details about your R environment like the search path, which packages are loaded, the version number of R, the locale, and the operating system of your computer. For example, here's what it outputs for my environment.

```
> sessionInfo()
```

```
R version 3.2.2 RC (2015-08-08 r68921)
Platform: x86_64-apple-darwin14.4.0 (64-bit)
Running under: OS X 10.10.4 (Yosemite)

locale:
[1] en_US.UTF-8/en_US.UTF-8/en_US.UTF-8/C/en_US.UTF-8/e\
n_US.UTF-8

attached base packages:
[1] stats     graphics  grDevices utils     datasets  b\
ase

other attached packages:
[1] knitr_1.10.5

loaded via a namespace (and not attached):
[1] magrittr_1.5  formatR_1.2  tools_3.2.2   stringi_0\
.5-5 stringr_1.0.0
[6] evaluate_0.7
```

Including a call to `sessionInfo()` at the end of each report written in R (perhaps with markdown or knitr) can be useful for communicating to the reader what type of environment is needed to reproduce the contents of the report (it may not be necessary but it's likely sufficient for simple analyses).

Don't Save Output

Saving output from various stages in a data analysis may seem like a responsible thing to do (what if the computer crashes), but it should be avoided if possible. The reason is that output files are often undocumented and the manner in which they were constructed can be difficult to reproduce. Better to save the inputs and code that were used to create a given piece of output rather than save the output itself. That way, if changes need to be made (or if output is lost), you can simply re-run the code with the appropriate input.

Outputs that you should avoid saving are things like tables, figures, summaries, and processed data. The one exception here is if it took a very long time to create that output. Then it might make sense to *temporarily* save some output for efficiency purposes. But in those cases, it's important to document carefully how the output was generated, perhaps via a version control system. Ultimately, if an output file cannot be easily connected with the means by which it was created, then it is not reproducible.

Set Your Seed

This is a niche issue that may not be generally applicable, but is often the source of non-reproducible results in statistical output or simulations. Many sophisticated statistical routines these days depend on the generation of random numbers. Think Markov chain Monte Carlo, random forests, and bootstrapping. Any procedure that depends on randomness will not generate the exact same output if you run it twice (the very definition of non-reproducibility). However, on a computer, random numbers are not truly random, rather they are pseudo-random. Therefore, it is possible to exactly reconstruct a sequence of pseudo-random numbers if you have the initial *seed*.

In R you can use the `set.seed()` function to set the random number generator seed and to specify which random number generator to use (see `?set.seed` for details). Setting the seed allows for the stream of random numbers to be exactly reproducible at a later date. Whenever you generate random numbers for a non-trivial purpose, **always set the seed** at the beginning of your code.

Here's an example of some random numbers.

```
> rnorm(5)
```

```
[1]  2.22414093  0.09524444 -1.16593756  0.59730725  1.\
34369099
```

There is now no way for me to go back (via code) and re-generate those numbers because I didn't set the seed. The next time I call `rnorm()` it will generate different numbers.

```
> rnorm(5)
```

```
[1] -1.9432379  0.6078967  1.8811491 -1.0447159  0.3690\
495
```

However, if I set the seed first, I can always re-generate the same numbers if needed.

```
> set.seed(10)
> rnorm(5)
```

```
[1]  0.01874617 -0.18425254 -1.37133055 -0.59916772  0.\
29454513
```

And again.

```
> set.seed(10)
> rnorm(5)
```

```
[1]  0.01874617 -0.18425254 -1.37133055 -0.59916772  0.\
29454513
```

Think About the Entire Pipeline

Data analysis is a lengthy process, starting from obtaining data all the way to generating results and communicating output. It is not just fitting a few prediction models or creating tables, figures, and reports. Typically, there will be raw data, processed or analytic data, analysis results, and then a final report. In addition to all that there will be code files that correspond to each of those transitions. They key thing to remember is that *how you got the end is just as important as the end itself*. The more of the *entire* data analysis pipeline you can make reproducible, the better for everyone (most importantly, yourself).

Summary

Here is the basic reproducibility check list:

- Are we doing good science?
- Was any part of this analysis done by hand? If so, are those parts *precisely* document? Does the documentation match reality?
- Have we taught a computer to do as much as possible (i.e. coded)?
- Are we using a version control system?
- Have we documented our software environment?
- Have we saved any output that we cannot reconstruct from original data + code?
- How far back in the analysis pipeline can we go before our results are no longer (automatically) reproducible?

Evidence-based Data Analysis

NOTE: Parts of this chapter were previously published on the *Simply Statistics*[42] blog.

Watch a video of this chapter: Part 1[43] Part 2[44] Part 3[45] Part 4[46] Part 5[47]

Discussions about reproducibility in scientific research have been on the rise lately. The rise in frequency of these discussions was in part a driver for me to write this book. There are many underlying trends that have produced this increased interest in reproducibility: larger and larger studies being harder to replicate independently, cheaper data collection technologies and methods producing larger datasets, cheaper computing power allowing for more sophisticated analyses (even for small datasets), and the rise of general computational science (for every "X" we now have "Computational X").

For those who are skipping around this book, here's a brief review of what I mean when I say "reproducibility". For the most part in science, we focus on what I and some others call "replication". The purpose of replication is to address the validity of a scientific claim. If I conduct a study and conclude that "X is related to Y", then others may be encouraged

---

[42] http://simplystatistics.org
[43] https://www.youtube.com/watch?v=Z792eZcBH3E
[44] https://www.youtube.com/watch?v=_gVgNkHRqu0
[45] https://www.youtube.com/watch?v=mzfVddVcYG0
[46] https://www.youtube.com/watch?v=1r98iJqlJtQ
[47] https://www.youtube.com/watch?v=jFDWhqKjk-o

to replicate my study—with independent investigators, data collection, instruments, methods, and analysis—in order to determine whether my claim of "X is related to Y" is in fact true. If many scientists replicate the study and come to the same conclusion, then there's evidence in favor of the claim's validity. If other scientists cannot replicate the same finding, then one might conclude that the original claim was false. In either case, this is how science has always worked and how it will continue to work.

Reproducibility, on the other hand, focuses on the validity of the data analysis. In the past, when datasets were small and the analyses were fairly straightforward, the idea of being able to reproduce a data analysis was perhaps not that interesting. But now, with computational science and big data, where data analyses can be extraodinarily complicated (and much of the value comes from the analysis), there's great interest in whether certain data analyses can in fact be reproduced. By this I mean is it possible to take someone's dataset and come to the same numerical/graphical/whatever output that they came to. While this seems theoretically trivial, in practice it's very complicated because a given data analysis, which typically will involve a long pipeline of analytic operations, may be difficult to keep track of without proper organization, training, or software.

What Problem Does Reproducibility Solve?

Reproducibility cannot really address the validity of a scientific claim as well as replication. Of course, if a given analysis is not reproducible, that may call into question any conclusions drawn from the analysis. However, if an analysis is reproducible, that says practically nothing about the validity of the conclusion or of the analysis itself.

In fact, there are numerous examples in the literature of analyses that were reproducible but just wrong. Perhaps the most nefarious recent example is the Potti scandal at Duke[48]. Given the amount of effort (somewhere close to 2000 hours) Keith Baggerly and his colleagues had to put into figuring out what Potti and others did, I think it's reasonable to say that their work was not reproducible. But in the end, Baggerly was able to reproduce some of the results–this was how he was able to figure out that the analysis were incorrect. If the Potti analysis had not been reproducible from the start, it would have been impossible for Baggerly to come up with the laundry list of errors that they made.

The Reinhart-Rogoff kerfuffle[49] is another example of analysis that ultimately was reproducible but nevertheless questionable. While Thomas Herndon did have to do a little reverse engineering to figure out the original analysis, it was nowhere near the years-long effort of Baggerly and colleagues. However, it was Reinhart-Rogoff's unconventional weighting scheme (fully reproducible, mind you) that drew all of the negative attention and strongly influenced the analysis.

I think the key question we want to answer when seeing the results of any data analysis is "Can I trust this analysis?" It's not possible to go into every data analysis and check everything, even if all the data and code were available. In most cases, we want to have a sense that the analysis was done appropriately (if not optimally). I would argue that requiring that analyses be reproducible does not address this key question.

With reproducibility you get a number of important bene-

---

[48] http://simplystatistics.org/2012/02/27/the-duke-saga-starter-set/
[49] http://simplystatistics.org/2013/04/19/podcast-7-reinhart-rogoff-reproducibility/

fits: transparency, data and code for others to analyze, and an increased rate of transfer of knowledge. These are all very important things. Data sharing in particular may be important independent of the need to reproduce a study if others want to aggregate datasets or do combined analyses. But **reproducibility does not guarantee validity or correctness of the analysis.**

Prevention vs. Medication

One key problem with the notion of reproducibility is the point in the research process at which we can apply it as an intervention. Reproducibility plays a role only in the most downstream aspect of the research process–post-publication. Only after a paper is published (and after any questionable analyses have been conducted) can we check to see if an analysis was reproducible or conducted in error.

At this point it may be difficult to correct any mistakes if they are identified. Grad students have graduated, postdocs have left, people have left the team. In the Potti case, letters to the journal editors were ignored. While it may be better to check the research process at the end rather than to never check it, intervening at the post-publication phase is arguably the most expensive place to do it. At this phase of the research process, you are merely "medicating" the problem, to draw an analogy with chronic diseases. But fundamental data analytic damage may have already been done.

This medication aspect of reproducibility reminds me of a famous quotation from R. A. Fisher:

> To consult the statistician after an experiment is finished is often merely to ask him to conduct

a post mortem examination. He can perhaps say what the experiment died of.

Reproducibility allows for the statistician to conduct the post mortem of a data analysis. But wouldn't it have been better to have prevented the analysis from dying in the first place?

Moving Upstream

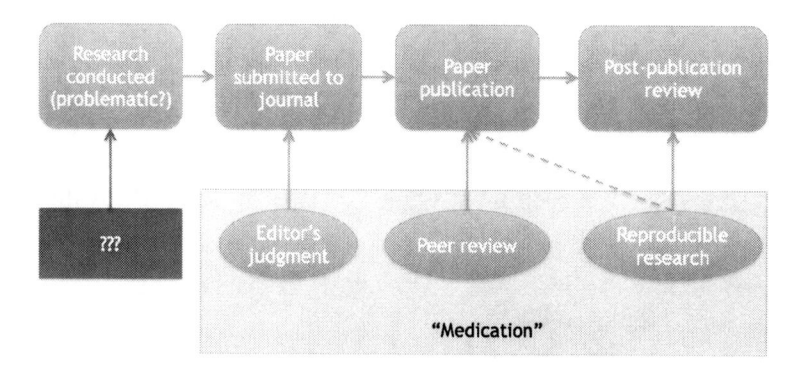

Reproducibility in the Publication Process?

There has already been much discussion of changing the role of reproducibility in the publication/dissemination process. What if a paper had to be deemed reproducible before it was published? The question here is who will reproduce the analysis? We can't trust the authors to do it so we have to get an independent third party. What about peer reviewers? I would argue that this is a pretty big burden to place on a peer reviewer who is already working for free. How about one of the Editors? Well, at the journal *Biostatistics*, that's exactly what we do. However, our policy is voluntary and only plays a role after a paper has been accepted through the usual peer review process. At any rate, from a business perspective, most journal owners will be reluctant to implement any policy that might reduce the number of submissions to the journal.

What Then?

To summarize, I believe reproducibility of computational research is very important, primarily to increase transparency and to improve knowledge sharing. However, I don't think reproducibility in and of itself addresses the fundamental question of "Can I trust this analysis?". Furthermore, reproducibility plays a role at the most downstream part of the research process (post-publication) where it is costliest to fix any mistakes that may be discovered. Ultimately, we need to think beyond reproducibility and to consider developing ways to ensure the quality of data analysis from the start.

How can we address the key problem concerning the validity of a data analysis?

Towards Evidence-based Data Analysis

Now, it's not true that reproducibility has no value. That's definitely not true and I'm hoping I can clarify my thinking in this followup post. Having code and data available, importantly, makes it possible to discover problems in an analysis, but only after the fact. I think this results in two issues: (1) It may take a while to figure out what exactly the problems are (even with code/data) and how to fix them; and (2) the problems in the analysis may have already caused some sort of harm.

Open Source Science?

For the first problem, I think a reasonable analogy for reproducible research is open source software. There the idea is that source code is available for all computer programs so that we can inspect and modify how a program runs. With open source software "all bugs are shallow". But the key here is that as long as all programmers have the requisite tools, they can modify the source code on their own, publish their corrected version (if they are fixing a bug), others can review it and accept or modify, and on and on. All programmers are more or less on the same footing, as long as they have the ability to hack the code. With distributed source code management systems like git, people don't even need permission to modify the source tree. In this environment, the best idea wins.

The analogy with open source software breaks down a bit with scientific research because not all players are on the same footing. Typically, the original investigator is much better equipped to modify the "source code", in this case the data analysis, and to fix any problems. Some types of analyses may require tremendous resources that are not available to all researchers. Also, it might take a long time for others who were not involved in the research, to fully understand what is going on and how to make reasonable modifications. That may involve, for example, learning the science in the first place, or learning how to program a computer for that matter. So I think making changes to a data analysis and having them accepted is a slow process in science, much more so than with open source software. There are definitely things we can do to improve our ability to make rapid changes/updates, but the implementation of those changes are only just getting started.

First Do No Harm

The second problem, that some sort of harm may have already occurred before an analysis can be fully examined is an important one. As I mentioned in the previous post, merely stating that an analysis is reproducible doesn't say a whole lot about whether it was done correctly. In order to verify that, someone knowledgeable has to go into the details and muck around to see what is going on. If someone is not available to do this, then we may never know what actually happened. Meanwhile, the science still stands and others may build off of it.

In the Duke saga, one of the most concerning aspects of the whole story was that some of Potti's research was going to be used to guide therapy in a clinical trial. The fact that a series of flawed data analyses was going to be used as the basis of choosing what cancer treatments people were going to get was very troubling. In particular, one of these flawed analyses reversed the labeling of the cancer and control cases!

To me, it seems that waiting around for someone like Keith Baggerly to come around and spend close to 2,000 hours reproducing, inspecting, and understanding a series of analyses is not an efficient system. In particular, when actual human lives may be affected, it would be preferable if the analyses were done right in the first place, without the "statistics police" having to come in and check that everything was done properly.

Evidence-based Data Analysis

What I think the statistical community needs to invest time and energy into is what I call "evidence-based data analysis".

What do I mean by this? Most data analyses are not the simple classroom exercises that we've all done involving linear regression or two-sample t-tests. Most of the time, you have to obtain the data, clean that data, remove outliers, impute missing values, transform variables and on and on, even before you fit any sort of model. Then there's model selection, model fitting, diagnostics, sensitivity analysis, and more. So a data analysis is really pipeline of operations where the output of one stage becomes the input of another.

The basic idea behind evidence-based data analysis is that for each stage of that pipeline, we should be using the best method, justified by appropriate statistical research that provides evidence favoring one method over another. If we cannot reasonable agree on a best method for a given stage in the pipeline, then we have a gap that needs to be filled. So we fill it!

Just to clarify things before moving on too far, here's a simple example.

Evidence-based Histograms

Consider the following simple histogram.

Histogram of x

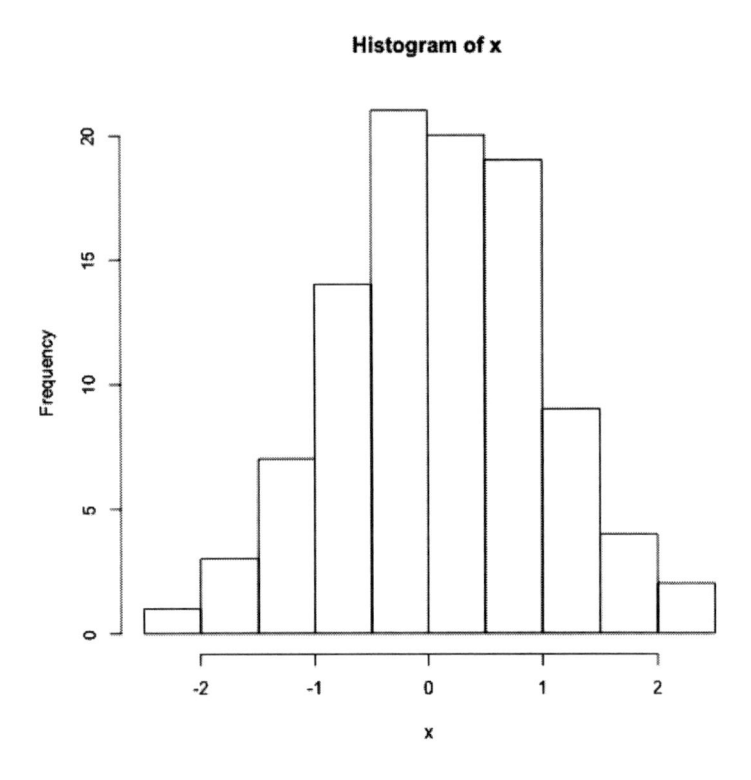

plot of chunk unnamed-chunk-2

The histogram was created in R by calling `hist(x)` on some Normal random deviates. Now, we all know that a histogram is a kind of smoother, and with any smoother, the critical parameter is the smoothing parameter or the bandwidth. Here, it's the size of the bin or the number of bins.

Notice that when I call `hist()` I don't actually specify the number of bins. Why not? Because in R, the default is to use Sturges' formula for the number of bins. Where does that come from? Well, there is a paper in the Journal of the American Statistical Association in 1926 by H. A. Sturges that justifies why such a formula is reasonable for a histogram (it is a very short paper, those were the days). R provides other choices for choosing the number of bins. For example, David Scott wrote a paper in Biometrika that justified bandwith/bin size based in integrated mean squared error criteria.

The point is that R doesn't just choose the default number of bins willy-nilly, there's actual research behind that choice and evidence supporting why it's a good choice. Now, we may not all agree that this default is the best choice at all times, but personally I rarely modify the default number of bins. Usually I just want to get a sense of what the distribution looks like and the default is fine. If there's a problem, transforming the variable somehow often is more productive than modifying the number of bins. What's the best transformation? Well, it turns out there's research on that too.

Evidence-based Reproducible Research

Now why can't we extend the idea behind the histogram bandwidth to all data analysis? I think we can. For every stage of a given data analysis pipeline, we can have the "best practices" and back up those practices with statistical research. Of course it's possible that such best practices have not yet been developed. This is common in emerging areas like genomics where the data collection technology is constantly changing. That's fine, but in more mature areas, I think it's possible for the community to agree on a series of practices that work, say, 90% of the time.

There are a few advantages to evidence-based reproducible research.

- It reduces the "researcher degrees of freedom". Researchers would be disincentivized from choosing the method that produces the "best" results if there is already a generally agreed upon approach. If a given data analysis required a different approach, the burden would be on the analyst to justify why a deviation from the generally accepted approach was made.
- The methodology would be transparent because the approach would have been vetted by the community. I call this "transparent box" analysis, as opposed to black box analysis. The analysis would be transparent so you would know exactly what is going on, but it would "locked in a box" so that you couldn't tinker with it to game the results.
- You would not have the lonely data analyst coming up with their own magical method to analyze the data. If a researcher claimed to have conducted an analysis using an evidence-based pipeline, you could at least have a sense that something reasonable was done. You would still need reproducibility to ensure that the researcher was not misrepresenting him/herself, but now we would have two checks on the analysis, not just one.
- Most importantly, evidence-based reproducible research attacks the furthest upstream aspect of the research, which is the analysis itself. It guarantees that generally accepted approaches are used to analyze the data from the very beginning and hopefully prevents problems from occurring rather than letting them propagate through the system.

Evidence-based Data Analysis in Practice

How can we implement evidence-based data analysis in practice? Depending on your favorite software system you could imagine a number of ways to do this. If the pipeline were implemented in R, you could imagine it as an R package. The precise platform is not critical at this point; I would imagine most complex pipelines would involve multiple different software systems tied together.

Below is a rough diagram of how I think the various pieces of an evidence-based data analysis pipeline would fit together.

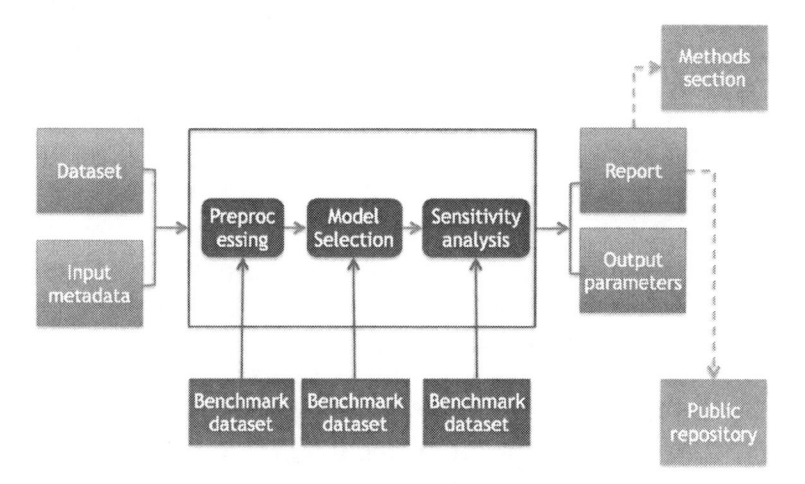

Deterministic Statistical Machine

There are a few key elements of this diagram that I'd like to stress:

- Inputs are minimal. You don't want to allow for a lot of inputs or arguments that can be fiddled with.

This reduces the number of degrees of freedom and hopefully reduces the amount of hacking. Basically, you want to be able to input the data and perhaps some metadata.
- Analysis comes in stages. There are multiple stages in any analysis, not just the part where you fit a model. Everything is important and every stage should use the best available method.
- The stuff in the red box does not involve manual intervention. The point is to not allow tweaking, fudging, and fiddling. Once the data goes in, we just wait for something to come out the other end.
- Methods should be benchmarked. For each stage of the analysis, there is a set of methods that are applied. These methods should, at a minimum, be benchmarked via a standard group of datasets. That way, if another method comes a long, we have an objective way to evaluate whether the new method is better than the older methods. New methods that improve on the benchmarks can replace the existing methods in the pipeline.
- Output includes a human-readable report. This report summarizes what the analysis was and what the results were (including results of any sensitivity analysis). The material in this report could be included in the "Methods" section of a paper and perhaps in the "Results" or "Supplementary Materials". The goal would be to allow someone who was not intimately familiar with the all of the methods used in the pipeline to be able to walk away with a report that he/she could understand and interpret. At a minimum, this person could take the report and share it with their local statistician for help with interpretation.
- There is a defined set of output parameters. Each anal-

ysis pipeline should, in a sense, have an "API" so that we know what outputs to expect (not the exact values, of course, but what kinds of values). For example, if a pipeline fits a regression model at the end the regression parameters are the key objects of interest, then the output could be defined as a vector of regression parameters. There are two reasons to have this: (1) the outputs, if the pipeline is deterministic, could be used for regression testing in case the pipeline is modified; and (2) the outputs could serve as inputs into another pipeline or algorithm.

Clearly, one pipeline is not enough. We need many of them for different problems. So what do we do with all of them?

I think we could organize them in a central location (kind of a specialized GitHub) where people could search for, download, create, and contribute to existing data analysis pipelines. An analogy (but not exactly a model) is the Cochrane Collaboration which serves as a repository for evidence-based medicine. There are already a number of initiatives along these lines, such as the Galaxy Project for bioinformatics. I don't know whether it'd be ideal to have everything in one place or have a number of sub-projects for specialized areas.

Each pipeline would have a leader (or "friendly dictator") who would organize the contributions and determine which components would go where. This could obviously be contentious, more some in some areas than in others, but I don't think any more contentious than your average open source project (check the archives of the Linus Kernel or Git mailing lists and you'll see what I mean).

Summary

To summarize, I think we need to organize lots of evidence-based data analysis pipelines and make them widely available. If I were writing this 5 or 6 years ago, I'd be complaining about a lack of infrastructure out there to support this. But nowadays, I think we have pretty much everything we need in terms of infrastructure. So what are we waiting for?

Public Reproducibility Resources

This chapter provides a list of resources that you may find useful when making your code and data available to others. The list is certainly incomplete, but provides a sense what what's out there. Keep in mind that all of these resources are primarily designed around making things *publicly* available. If you do not want the public to access your material, you may need to seek other resources (or pay a fee).

Code Repositories

- GitHub[50]: this site hosts git repositories for free if they are public and for a fee if they are private. GitHub offers a lot of features for collaborating with others such as the ability to track issues and for others to merge changes into your repository. Hosting a repository here typically obviates the need for a separate mailing list as many of the communication aspects are built in.
- Sourceforge[51]: An older site that similarly hosts code repositories including those based on Mercurial, git, or subversion. Features also include issue tracking and discussion forums.
- Bitbucket[52]: similar to other sites described above, Bitbucket hosts repositories based on Mercurial or git

---

[50] https://github.com
[51] http://sourceforge.net
[52] https://bitbucket.org

and allows for simple collaboration between project team members. Pricing is based on the number of users collaborating on a repository. They also have a special plan for academics (if you have a .edu email address).
- repo.or.cz[53]: this site was one of the original repositories for hosting git repositories. It is free, and is still running, but has largely been overtaken by other sites like GitHub, which offer far more in the way of features.
- CRAN[54]: this is the central repository for R packages. If you develop code for R, in addition to hosting your source code on a site like GitHub, it's probably wise to put a package on CRAN so that others can easily install it.

It may be logical to host data in a code repository, if the datasets are small and manageable (typically "toy" datasets or demonstration datasets). Large datasets are usually not suitable for hosting in a code repository.

Data Repositories

- NCBI[55]: The National Center for Biotechnology Information hosts a number of databases to which you can upload data for scientific publications and from which you can obtain publicly available data. It is an enormous resource for biological data and the go-to place for biological researchers looking to deposit their data.

---
[53] http://repo.or.cz
[54] http://cran.r-project.org
[55] http://www.ncbi.nlm.nih.gov

- Dataverse[56]: This site is run out of Harvard's Institute for Quantitative and Social Science as a place where researchers can host their data with their papers. Datasets get a permanent unique ID that can be referenced elsewhere.
- ICPSR[57]: The Inter-university Consortium for Political and Social Research is another repository for datasets, typically in the social sciences.

Publication Repositories

- R Pubs[58]: this is a fairly simple web site hosted by RStudio[59] that allows for the simple publication of HTML documents created using the RStudio development environment. If you are creating an R markdown document in RStudio, you can, with the click of a button, publish the HTML version of that document to RPubs and immediately make it publicly available. RPubs will provide you with a permanent unique link that you can share with others.
- GitHub[60]: Although GitHub is a source code repository, it can be quite useful for hosting documents too. In particular, the web site will automatically interpret markdown documents and prettify them so that people can view the directly from the repository in their web browser.

---

[56] http://dataverse.org
[57] https://www.icpsr.umich.edu/icpsrweb/landing.jsp
[58] http://rpubs.com
[59] https://www.rstudio.com
[60] https://github.com